European
LUXURY HOME PLANS

*Introducing
65 Sater European-style
Home Plans*

Photograph by: Joseph Lapeyra

Fred and Delores Sater

In Memory

When I think about influences in my life, I can't help but remember my "Grandpa Sater." He influenced me more than he could have imagined. It wasn't for the great things he accomplished, for by the world's standards he would receive little acknowledgement; but it was the little things he did that made him a giant in my world. His quiet and gentle manner reflected a man who loved and cared for his grandchildren, never too busy to listen to your stories and always ready to share a corny joke.

He also loved building homes. He took great pride in making sure each home was crafted and detailed to give many years of enjoyment to its owners. His ideology and vision influenced my own as I sought to create the very best designs possible. This collection is dedicated to my grandfather and his inspiration and love of home building.

Dan F. Sater II

Plan 8022 - Italian-style courtyard

A DESIGNS DIRECT PUBLISHING BOOK

Presented by

The Sater Design Collection, Inc.
The Center at the Springs
25241 Elementary Way, Suite 201, Bonita Springs, FL 34135

Dan F. Sater, II — *CEO and Author*

Amy Fullwiler — *Editor-in-Chief*

Laura Hurst Brown — *Editor*

Dave Jenkins — *Illustrator*

Diane J. Zwack — *Art Director*

Kim Campeau — *Graphic Artist*

CONTRIBUTING PHOTOGRAPHERS

Dan Forer, Tom Harper, Joesph Lapeyra, Kim Sargent, Doug Thompson and C.J. Walker

Front Cover Photo: Tom Harper & Doug Thompson / *Back Cover Photo:* C.J. Walker

Printed by: Toppan Printing Co., Hong Kong

First Printing, October 2003

10 9 8 7 6 5 4 3 2

TABLE OF | *Contents*

Photograph by: C.J. Walker

a diversity of cultural influence

Photograph by: C.J. Walker

Sater Design | PHILOSOPHY

In creating this series of designs, my intent was not so much to replicate European designs as to capture the essence of classical beauty inherent in each archetype. Classical old-world architecture greatly influenced early American residential design in many ways. Admirers of great masters such as Thomas Jefferson brought back these ideas and eagerly sought to incorporate them into a truly American style. It is with this same passion that we bring you **"European Luxury Home Plans,"** a new-world portfolio of distinctly American homes—representing not replicas but truly new designs that borrow from the character and magic of these masterpieces. We have integrated these history-rich exteriors with plans that include all of the up-to-the-minute conveniences and amenities one would expect in a modern American home.

I have selected four regions of European influence: Italian, French, English and Spanish. Each of these played an important role in the development of American residential design. Allow me to explain the varied styles and influences of each area as it translates into colonial and later periods.

ITALIAN

No country has more profoundly influenced residential architecture than Italy. Great masters such as Vignola, Palladio and Bernini employed great skill in practicing their craft. No one, however, impacted residential design like Palladio. Andrea Palladio compiled his designs and ideas into a series of books on architecture. He set guidelines for scale and proportion in the designs of facades, massing and interiors. More importantly, it was Palladio who best achieved

the new union between the classical and vernacular traditions that shaped much of the modern architecture of Western Europe. His concepts have continued to affect not only the design of homes but of cities as well, both in Europe and America.

Plan 8057 - Italian-style master bath

Palladio also understood the relationship between home and site. Jefferson fully explored this important link with the design of "Monticello," which aptly means "little hill." This marriage of the house to the landscape demonstrates that good design doesn't compete with its site, it completes it.

Classical architects also understood the relationship of the home to its occupants. In fact, classical architecture may be construed as an embodiment of the human form, seeking to relate building proportions to human scale. The

Italians, in particular, developed a mastery of these techniques. American styles that reflect direct Italian influences are Renaissance, Tuscan and Baroque.

FRENCH

French architecture extended the concepts of scale and site relative to houses with a heightened sense

Plan 8001 - French-style study

of grandeur and luxe detail. Residential design reached its greatest heights under the tutelage of French kings who, impressed by Italian life and art, sought to emulate the rich aesthetics and translate them into a truly French style. Great French architects such as Philibert de l'Orme and Jacques Androuet du Cerceau, and later Francois Mansart, defined this style by focusing on the use of ornament over form. French kings and the "nouveaux riche" built many grand mansions, incorporating art as architecture and adding new features such as porte-cocheres, galleries and grand staircases. The

use of steeply pitched roofs punctuated with numerous dormers became a common element in crowning French homes. The use of columns divorced from arches were also a departure from the Roman influence, and became an important part of French classical architecture.

American styles that reflect French influences are Chateauesque, Beaux Arts, French Provincial (Country) and Second Empire.

ENGLISH

England was also greatly influenced by the Italian design aesthetics as well as, to a lesser extent, French architecture. Yet British architects such as Inigo Jones and his contemporaries developed their own unique style by implementing Palladian concepts with a decidedly British flair. An important part of the English contribution were the country houses of the 16th and 17th centuries.

Aside from the obvious, it is easy to understand the direct English influence on American architecture. With transcontinental waves of immigrants came a wealth of variants on the dominant British styles. Benjamin Latrobe, the first professional architect to practice in America, was born in Yorkshire and trained in London. He drew plans for the White House and other notable public buildings, and later influenced a generation of leading American designers.

The use of architectural or plan books became a common way of translating ideas to the new world. One such book reflecting the works of James Gibbs was greatly copied in the Colonies.

American styles influenced by the British Isles are Georgian, Colonial Revival, Gothic (Tudor), Victorian and Classical Revival, to name a few.

a heightened sense of grandeur

Photograph by: C.J. Walker

thoughtful intimate spaces

Photograph by: Joseph Lapeyra

SPANISH

Spain's role in American residential design may be seen in the houses of the Southwest and, to a lesser extent, in the coastal regions of Florida, where Spanish rule lasted for centuries. Spanish architecture was influenced not only by elements of Italian and French design, but by Moorish styles as well. Coupled with Native American building techniques, the eclectic dialects of the Spanish vernacular led to a truly unique archetype in home design.

Islamic influences altered the home's relationship with nature, with such residential features as courtyards, interior fountains and arched loggias, or porches. The use of brightly colored tile mosaics for decoration on sculpted stucco and stone facades extended the Spanish vernacular and is practiced with artful skill in modern revivals. The Spanish also first introduced the horseshoe arch, a unique architectural form.

Romanesque architecture also flourished in Spain. Its simple yet bold geometries together with the extensive use of the Roman arch is easily translated into new world architecture. Its eclectic blends and bold shapes are still in great demand in American residential design today.

American styles that reflect Spanish influences are Mediterranean, Spanish Colonial and Monterey.

In closing, what makes America great is its diversity of people, cultures and influences. This diversity is profoundly seen in our architectural heritage. It is also our freedom in combining these influences that serves to develop truly American architectural translations of residential design. As Americans, we tend to romanticize our notions of history. We look to larger-than-life images of heroes of the wild frontier, such as Daniel Boone and Buffalo Bill. We even recreate utopia-like experiences of our hometown, such as Disney's "Main Street," all to enhance our memories and make them seem even better than we remember. Our efforts to create an ever-better vision of the American dream is also part of our heritage, and so what is to come will undoubtedly reflect our past.

I hope you will find in these home plans a sense of that great heritage not only in timeless exterior elevations but also in well-planned interiors that

Plan 8052 - Spanish-style hallway

incorporate thoughtful intimate spaces with ultra-functional modern amenities. I hope that you and your family will find in these pages the home of your American dream.

May God grant his blessings of peace, prosperity and joy to your home and all who reside within!

Dan F. Sater II, AIBD, CPBD

The clean, uncompromised aesthetics of classic Western European style offer a timeless quality that most Americans can easily recognize. Indeed, the artful proportions and perfect scale of places like Monticello are an integral, unmistakable part of our past. More than that, the architectural legacies of ancient cultures such as Rome and Greece have

Plan 8009 - English-style kitchen

emerged—translated in idiosyncratic ways—in the town neighborhoods throughout our young history.

Influenced by such diverse cultural fare as fashion and economics, styles here have evolved in a particularly intimate way. Americans push back convention with regional styles that transcribe their ancestral vernaculars—in order to find a comfortable refuge. Rarely do they turn away from historical precedent. Instead, transitional styles take root and grow across generations of owners, taking on the future with a timelessness of their own.

Eclectic designs evolved from the pure forms of a remote past please us, even today. The hooded windows and sculpted cornices of Italianate plans, derived from rural Italian folk houses, grew out of the 19th-century picturesque dialect in Europe. Decorative details borrowed from the Moors find rich partnerships with cantilevered balconies and breezy courtyards in Spanish revival homes. The rough-faced stonework and powerful shapes of modern Romanesque villas are layered with history.

Still, it is hardly a finely turned streetscape that calls a rebellious spirit home. Ultra-busy, three-income families speak to designers not in terms of ageless lines, scale and proportion, but of their everyday lives: when their children go to bed, how they entertain and what they make for breakfast. And while the outside of the house will remind them of who they are, the interior spaces must invisibly support their individual preferences.

Houses are abstract. At their inception, they are mere lines on a page. How a house functions stretches its architecture, and confirms it. Forms that don't shelter, inspire and nurture us, soon become relics to be studied, not lived in. In this book are residential plans that reflect our heritage, that call up true spatial relationships and a classic sense of proportion. Each room, each plan, and how one feels in it, is a measure of its beauty. These designs were created, not to a grand scale, but relate to a human scale, and to nature.

form paired with decorative detail

REGION/STYLE | *Italian*

Renaissance, Rococo, Villa and Tuscan—

here are houses with dramatic exteriors of raised porches and pedimented porticos.

Retreating walls and luxe outdoor amenities

create modern living environments that evoke qualities of the

rural folk houses of Venice.

Here are homes that remember how fresh breezes

weave silently into the textures of a room, and moonlight finds its way

past a portico or into a courtyard.

Photograph by: Dan Forer

Italian | RENAISSANCE VILLA

© The Sater Design Collection, Inc.

Alessandra

PALAZZO VIENNA — *Grace flows through this stylish villa like a subtle motif— from its celestial entry to its wide-open veranda—with the promise of true respite.*

Massive square columns frame a spectacular portico and pedimented window above the entry of this romantic villa—influenced by renaissance forms and an elegant introduction to its splendid and livable interior. Well-defined formal rooms designed for planned events offer both intimacy and grandeur, while the casual zone provides a lose-the-shoes atmosphere that's deeply relaxing. Defined by a series of sculpted arches, the central corridor extends the plan's sight lines to the leisure and master wings, and accepts sunlight through a turret of tall windows. Double doors lead from the stair hall to a quiet study, which shares a through-fireplace with the living room and opens to the veranda. On the upper level, a balcony hall benefits from windows to the front and rear of the plan, connecting secondary and guest quarters that boast private decks.

PLAN | *8003*

Bedroom: 4   Width: 85'0"

Bath: 3-1/2   Depth: 76'8"

Foundation: Slab or
  optional basement

Exterior Walls: 2x6

Main Level: 2,815 sq ft

Upper Level: 1,130 sq ft

Living Area: 3,945 sq ft

Price Code: **L1**

Veranda
12'-6" Clg.

Leisure Room
20'-8" x 19'-1"
11'-0" to 12'-0"
Coffered Clg.

Nook
9'-6" to 10'-0"
Stepped Clg.

Veranda
20'-0" Clg.

Master Suite
14'-10" x 20'-6"
12'-0" to 10'-8"
Stepped Clg.

Kitchen
13'-2" x 20'-0"
9'-6" to 10'-0"
Stepped Clg.

Living Room
16'-0" x 14'-4"
Open to Above

Study
11'-2" x 12'-8"
10'-0" Clg.

WIC   WIC

Utility
10'-0" Clg.

Pass-Thru

2 Sided Fireplace

Pantry

Art Niche

Gallery
10'-0" Clg.

Bench

Walk-In Shower

Powder Bath

Art Niche

Garage
21'-2" x 34'-10"
10'-0" clg.

Dining
12'-10" x 13'-0"
10'-0" Clg.

Grand Foyer
Open to Above

Master Bath
10'-0" Clg.

Entry
10'-10" Clg.

Whirlpool

©THE SATER DESIGN
COLLECTION, INC.

main level

WIC   **Deck**

©THE SATER DESIGN
COLLECTION, INC.

Deck

Bedroom 3
12'-10" x 15'-2"
8'-8" Clg.

Open to Below
19'-8" to 20'-0"
Coffered Clg.

Guest Suite
11'-2" x 19'-8"
8'-8" Clg.

Walk-In Shower

Bath 2   Walk-In Shower

WIC

Bath 3

Balcony
8'-8" Clg.

WIC   Attic Access

Bedroom 2
12'-6" x 12'-10"
10'-8" Clg.

Plant Shelf

Open to Below

Balcony

upper level

rear elevation

www.saterdesign.com

© The Sater Design Collection, Inc.

© The Sater Design Collection, Inc.

Chadbryne

COOL HAVEN — *An artful disposition evokes the charm of a hillside castello—bold yet simple, elegant and strong—and offers plenty of outdoor places.*

Stacked stone and stucco capture the character of a rural Italian manor, influenced by the pastoral forms of Tuscany. Cast-stone elements offset the hand-glazed sunshine hues of the stucco facade. Fanlights, transoms and shapely balustrades highlight two bold turrets, rustic and smooth, which harbor a bay window and a wraparound portico. The glass-paneled entry announces an open foyer enhanced by square columns and arches, framing spectacular interior vistas that extend to the veranda and rear yard. Architectural details—a coffered ceiling above the two-story great room, an art niche and built-in cabinetry—contribute in subtle ways to the decor. Commercial-quality appliances in the kitchen and a computer loft upstairs play counterpoint to rough-hewn ceiling beams and rugged stone accents in the breakfast nook and study.

PLAN | *8004*

Bedroom: 4   Width: 91'0"

Bath: 3-1/2   Depth: 52'8"

Foundation: Slab or
  optional basement

Exterior Walls: 2x6

Main Level: 2,219 sq ft

Upper Level: 1,085 sq ft

Living Area: 3,304 sq ft

Bonus Room: 404 sq ft

Price Code: **C4**

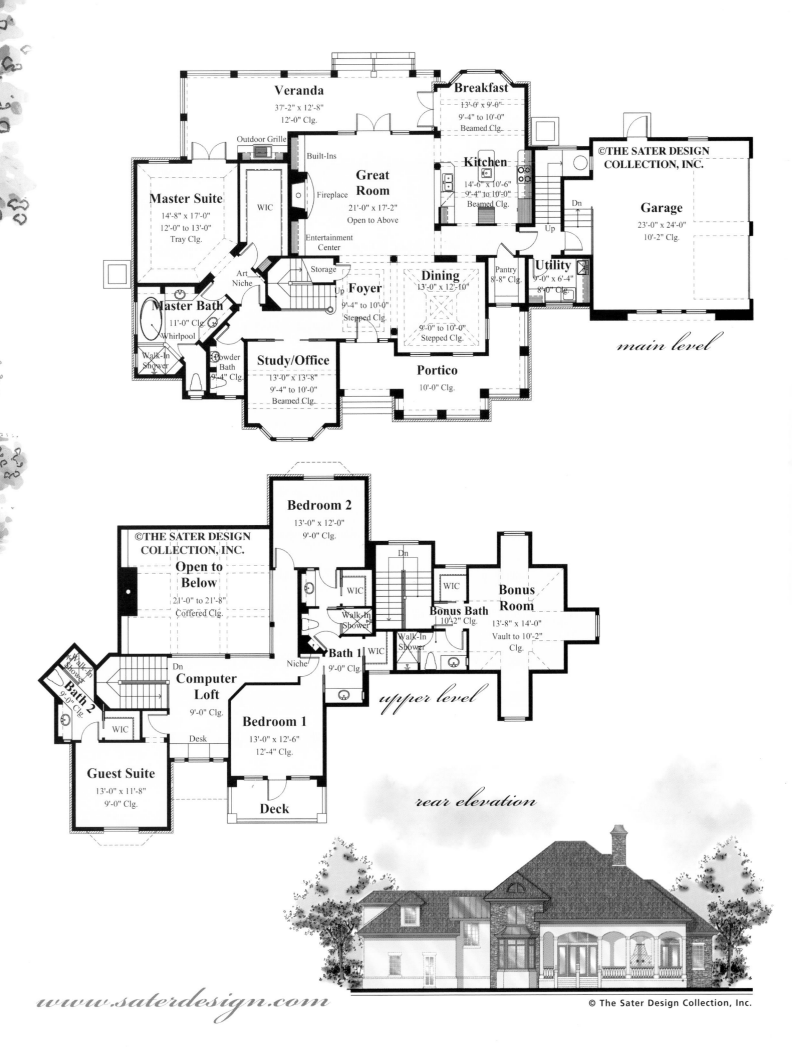

Veranda
37'-2" x 12'-8"
12'-0" Clg.

Breakfast
13'-0" x 9'-0"
9'-4" to 10'-0"
Beamed Clg.

Outdoor Grille

Built-Ins

Kitchen
14'-6" x 10'-6"
9'-4" to 10'-0"
Beamed Clg.

©THE SATER DESIGN
COLLECTION, INC.

Master Suite
14'-8" x 17'-0"
12'-0" to 13'-0"
Tray Clg.

WIC

Fireplace

**Great
Room**
21'-0" x 17'-2"
Open to Above

Dn

Garage
23'-0" x 24'-0"
10'-2" Clg.

Entertainment
Center

Art
Niche

Storage

Up

Foyer
9'-4" to 10'-0"
Stepped Clg.

Dining
13'-0" x 12'-10"
9'-0" to 10'-0"
Stepped Clg.

Pantry
8'-8" Clg.

Utility
9'-0" x 6'-4"
8'-0" Clg.

Up

Master Bath
11'-0" Clg.

Whirlpool

Walk-In
Shower

Powder
Bath
9'-4" Clg.

Study/Office
13'-0" x 13'-8"
9'-4" to 10'-0"
Beamed Clg.

Portico
10'-0" Clg.

main level

Bedroom 2
13'-0" x 12'-0"
9'-0" Clg.

©THE SATER DESIGN
COLLECTION, INC.

**Open to
Below**
21'-0" to 21'-8"
Coffered Clg.

WIC

Dn

WIC

Bonus Room
13'-8" x 14'-0"
Vault to 10'-2"
Clg.

Walk-In
Shower

Bonus Bath
10'-2" Clg.

Walk-In
Shower

Bath 2
9'-0" Clg.

Walk-In
Shower

**Computer
Loft**
9'-0" Clg.

Dn

Niche

Bath 1
9'-0" Clg.

WIC

upper level

WIC

Desk

Bedroom 1
13'-0" x 12'-6"
12'-4" Clg.

Guest Suite
13'-0" x 11'-8"
9'-0" Clg.

Deck

rear elevation

www.saterdesign.com

© The Sater Design Collection, Inc.

Italian | VILLA

Della Porta

SUNSHINE STATE — *Contemporary lines play counterpoint to ancient curves and a colonial provenance—wrapped with windows and a distinctly cheerful personality.*

Carved brackets and balusters, stucco, glass panels and shingles surround a triple-arch entry—a grand start for this spacious villa. Designed for 21st-century living, the interior plan creates elegant, flexible spaces that are not formal or self-conscious, but simply comfortable. Defined by arches, columns and magnificent views that extend beyond the rambling veranda, the central living room opens to the dining room and shares a two-sided fireplace with the study. The well-organized conversation kitchen takes in natural light through the retreating glass walls of the leisure room and the morning bay. Gatherings large and small may spill out onto the veranda—where a complete outdoor kitchen facilitates meals alfresco. A stepped ceiling highlights the master suite, a spectacular retreat for two owners.

PLAN | *8007*

Bedroom: 3   Width: 106'4"
Bath: 3-1/2   Depth: 102'4"
Foundation: Slab or
    optional basement
Exterior Walls: 2x6

Main Level: 3,640 sq ft

Living Area: 3,640 sq ft

Price Code: **L1**

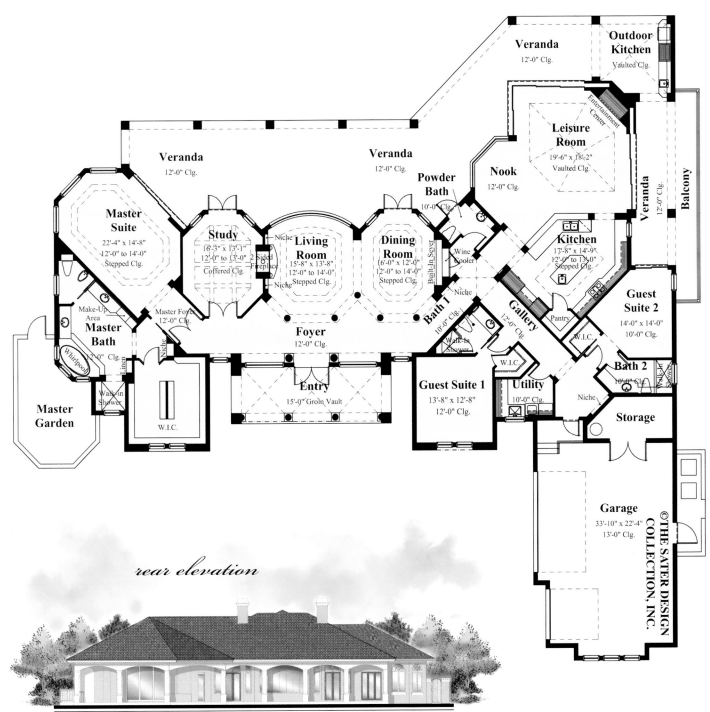

rear elevation

© The Sater Design Collection, Inc.

with walkout basement

© The Sater Design Collection, Inc.

www.saterdesign.com

© The Sater Design Collection, Inc.

Capucina

NEW WORLD — *Rich with romantic elements evocative of a Tuscan villa, this refined yet rugged elevation conveys the sense of a rambling country home evolved over time.*

Stone gables complement a sculpted entry enhanced by elaborate glass panels and a detailed fanlight at the front of this stunning Italian Country manor. Cream-white stucco reinforced with bold masonry, pilasters and crowns express an ancient architecture that carves an elegant profile in 21st-century new neighborhoods. The central turret window harbors an interior plant shelf framed by a triple skylight overlooking the foyer. An open arrangement of the central living space, gallery and formal dining room permits great views of the back property through a two-story bow window. French doors open the leisure room to the outdoors, while the morning bay grants access to a lanai shared with the master suite's private sitting bay. Upstairs, a balcony hall—with views of the foyer and living room—connects the family bedrooms and guest quarters with ample attic storage.

PLAN | *8010*

Bedroom: 4   Width: 71'6"

Bath: 4-1/2   Depth: 83'0"

Foundation: Slab or
   optional basement

Exterior Walls: 2x6

Main Level: 2,850 sq ft

Upper Level: 1,155 sq ft

Living Area: 4,005 sq ft

Bonus Room: 371 sq ft

Price Code: **L1**

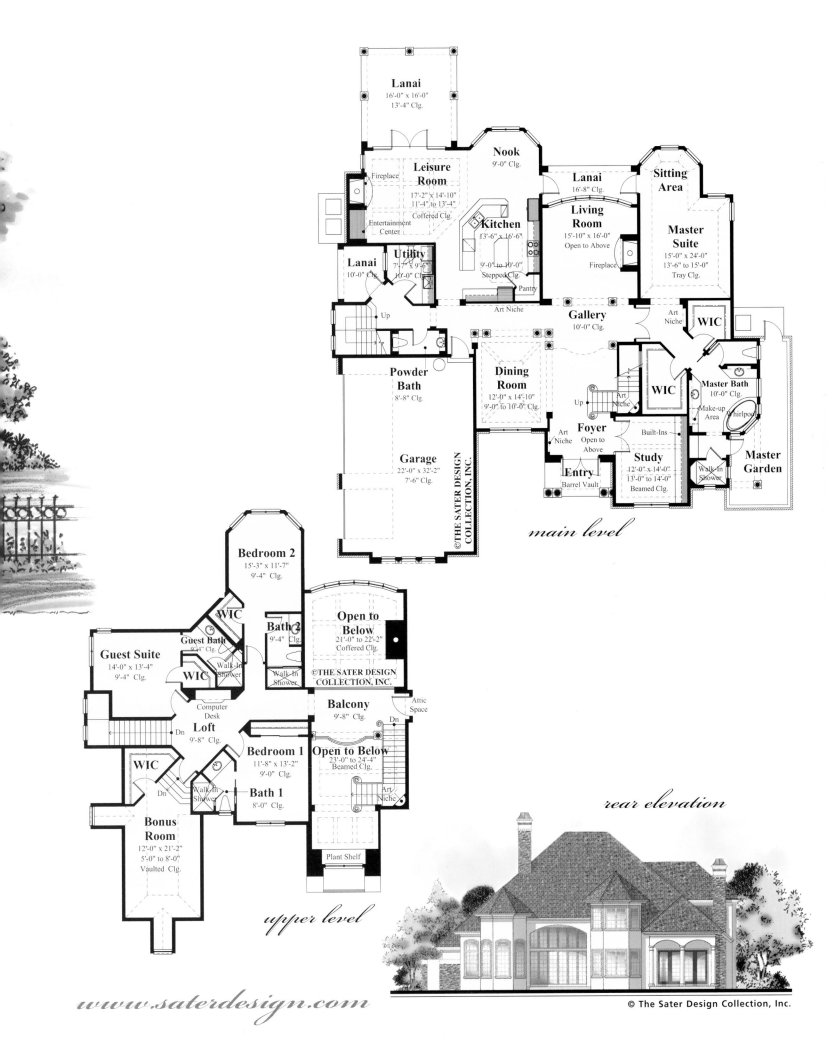

Lanai
16'-0" x 16'-0"
13'-4" Clg.

Leisure Room
17'-2" x 14'-10"
11'-4" to 13'-4"
Coffered Clg.

Fireplace

Nook
9'-0" Clg.

Lanai
16'-8" Clg.

Sitting Area

Entertainment Center

Kitchen
13'-6" x 16'-6"
9'-0" to 10'-0"
Stepped Clg.

Living Room
15'-10" x 16'-0"
Open to Above

Master Suite
15'-0" x 24'-0"
13'-6" to 15'-0"
Tray Clg.

Lanai
10'-0" Clg.

Utility
7'-7" x 9'-6"
10'-0" Clg.

Fireplace

Pantry

Art Niche

Gallery
10'-0" Clg.

Art Niche

WIC

Up

Powder Bath
8'-8" Clg.

Dining Room
12'-0" x 14'-10"
9'-0" to 10'-0"

Up

Art Niche

WIC

Master Bath
10'-0" Clg.

Make-up Area

Whirlpool

Garage
22'-0" x 32'-2"
7'-6" Clg.

Art Niche

Foyer
Open to Above

Built-Ins

Study
12'-0" x 14'-0"
13'-0" to 14'-0"
Beamed Clg.

Walk-In Shower

Master Garden

Entry
Barrel Vault

©THE SATER DESIGN COLLECTION, INC.

main level

Bedroom 2
15'-3" x 11'-7"
9'-4" Clg.

WIC

Guest Bath
9'-4" Clg.

Bath 2
9'-4" Clg.

Walk-In Shower

Open to Below
21'-0" to 22'-2"
Coffered Clg.

Guest Suite
14'-0" x 13'-4"
9'-4" Clg.

WIC

Walk-In Shower

©THE SATER DESIGN COLLECTION, INC.

Computer Desk

Attic Space

WIC

Loft
9'-8" Clg.

Dn

Balcony
9'-8" Clg.

Dn

Bedroom 1
11'-8" x 13'-2"
9'-0" Clg.

Open to Below
23'-0" to 24'-4"
Beamed Clg.

Walk-In Shower

Dn

Bath 1
8'-0" Clg.

Art Niche

Bonus Room
12'-0" x 21'-2"
5'-0" to 8'-0"
Vaulted Clg.

Plant Shelf

upper level

rear elevation

© The Sater Design Collection, Inc.

www.saterdesign.com

© The Sater Design Collection, Inc.

San Lorenzo

MASTER PLAN — *Revival elements—quoins, fractables and sculpted masonry surrounds—recall the breathtaking beauty of authentic rural Italian villas.*

Massive stone pilasters guard a paneled entry and stair tower, which break the forward massing of this European design. Round clerestory windows and keystones bring a sweet familiarity to a facade that's bold enough to be called "brand new." A coffered ceiling and a two-story bow window brighten the core of the plan: the living room, which shares a two-sided fireplace with the study. The formal dining room brags texture enlivened by natural light, with a stepped ceiling and rusticated walls—and views and vistas all around. The foyer and central gallery benefit from the spectacular stairway that winds through the turret, linking the hall with a balcony loft. An open arrangement of the leisure room and kitchen permits breezes and a sense of nature to circulate through the entire wing. Ceiling beams unify the space with the extensive computer loft, and echo the terraced ceiling of the veranda.

PLAN | *8014*

Bedroom: 4   Width: 70'0"

Bath: 4-1/2   Depth: 100'0"

Foundation: Slab or
   optional basement

Exterior Walls: 2x6

Main Level: 3,025 sq ft

Upper Level: 1,639 sq ft

Living Area: 4,664 sq ft

Bonus Room: 294 sq ft

Price Code: **L2**

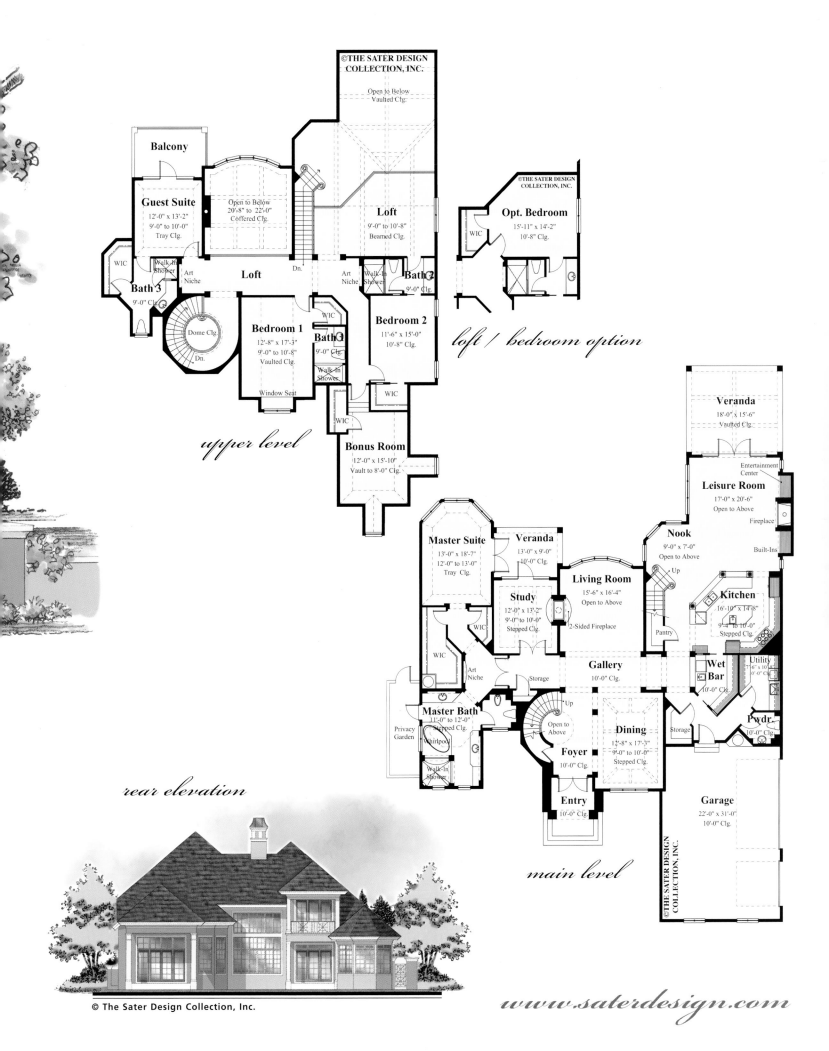

©THE SATER DESIGN
COLLECTION, INC.

Open to Below
Vaulted Clg.

Balcony

Guest Suite
12'-0" x 13'-2"
9'-0" to 10'-0"
Tray Clg.

Open to Below
20'-8" x 22'-0"
Coffered Clg.

Loft
9'-0" to 10'-8"
Beamed Clg.

©THE SATER DESIGN
COLLECTION, INC.

Opt. Bedroom
15'-11" x 14'-2"
10'-8" Clg.

WIC

WIC

Walk-In
Shower

Art
Niche

Loft

Dn.

Art
Niche

Walk-In
Shower

Bath 2
9'-0" Clg.

Bath 3
9'-0" Clg.

Dome Clg.

Dn.

Bedroom 1
12'-8" x 17'-3"
9'-0" to 10'-8"
Vaulted Clg.

WIC

Bath
9'-0" Clg.

Walk-In
Shower

Bedroom 2
11'-6" x 15'-0"
10'-8" Clg.

loft / bedroom option

WIC

Window Seat

WIC

upper level

WIC

Bonus Room
12'-0" x 15'-10"
Vault to 8'-0" Clg.

Veranda
18'-0" x 15'-6"
Vaulted Clg.

Entertainment
Center

Leisure Room
17'-0" x 20'-6"
Open to Above

Fireplace

Built-Ins

Master Suite
13'-0" x 18'-7"
12'-0" to 13'-0"
Tray Clg.

Veranda
13'-0" x 9'-0"
10'-0" Clg.

Nook
9'-0" x 7'-0"
Open to Above

Living Room
15'-6" x 16'-4"
Open to Above

Up

Study
12'-0" x 13'-2"
9'-0" to 10'-0"
Stepped Clg.

Kitchen
16'-10" x 14'-8"
9'-4" to 10'-0"
Stepped Clg.

WIC

2-Sided Fireplace

Pantry

WIC

Art
Niche

Storage

Gallery
10'-0" Clg.

**Wet
Bar**
10'-0" Clg.

Utility
7'-6" x 10'
10'-0" Clg.

Up

Open to
Above

Master Bath
11'-0" to 12'-0"
Stepped Clg.

Privacy
Garden

Whirlpool

Open to
Above

Storage

Dining
12'-8" x 17'-3"
9'-0" to 10'-0"
Stepped Clg.

Pwdr.
10'-0" Clg.

Walk-In
Shower

Foyer
10'-0" Clg.

Garage
22'-0" x 31'-0"
10'-0" Clg.

rear elevation

Entry
10'-0" Clg.

main level

©THE SATER DESIGN
COLLECTION, INC.

© The Sater Design Collection, Inc.

www.saterdesign.com

© The Sater Design Collection, Inc.

Vienna

EARTH AND SKY — *Rugged stone walls, shapely balusters and rough-hewn wood shutters set the tone for this historic design—drawn from 13th-century lines for lifestyles of today.*

A dialogue between tradition and innovation, the Old World elements of this striking facade belie a form-and-function interior packed with new-century amenities. Parallel wings harbor private and public realms, connected by an airy great room and gallery-style foyer at the heart of the home. An extended-hearth fireplace shares its beauty with spaces of the informal zone—the food-preparation area of the gourmet kitchen, and the morning nook. Wraparound counters, a walk-in pantry and shelf space in the servery area of the kitchen facilitate planned events. Bay windows brighten the master wing, granting views of the front property from the study, and vistas of the back property from the owners' bedroom. A forward sun porch on the upper level extends natural light to the balcony loft, which links two secondary bedroom suites and guest quarters.

PLAN | *8020*

Bedroom: 4 Width: 80'0"

Bath: 4-1/2 Depth: 63'8"

Foundation: Slab or
 optional basement

Exterior Walls: 2x6

Main Level: 2,232 sq ft

Upper Level: 1,269 sq ft

Living Area: 3,501 sq ft

Price Code: **L1**

Bartolini

SUN DANCE — *Trefoil windows and a deeply sculpted portico set off a lyrical Mediterranean aesthetic inspired by 15th-century forms and an oceanfront attitude.*

A graceful entry arcade set off by massive stucco arches, classic pilasters and a groin-vaulted ceiling leads to a grand foyer arrayed with elaborate sculptural forms. Three sets of French doors open the great room to a garden veranda and to a courtyard that meanders around a circular fountain, forming a broad promenade rich with greenery. Sculpted arches, carved wood and ceramic tile create a subtly ornamented interior, framed by breezy outdoor views. The forward rooms establish a formal zone enhanced by a variety of architectural elements, including projecting bays, deeply carved arches, and coffered and beamed ceilings. A private wing that includes the kitchen and morning nook opens to a covered loggia, lounge and grille. The secluded master suite provides its own access to the courtyard, while the upper level harbors two secondary suites, a loft and a bonus room with a bay tower.

PLAN | *8022*

Bedroom: 3   Width: 60'6"
Bath: 2-1/2   Depth: 94'0"
Foundation: Slab or
    optional basement
Exterior Walls: 2x6

Main Level: 2,084 sq ft
Upper Level: 652 sq ft

Living Area: 2,736 sq ft
Bonus Room: 375 sq ft

Price Code: **C3**

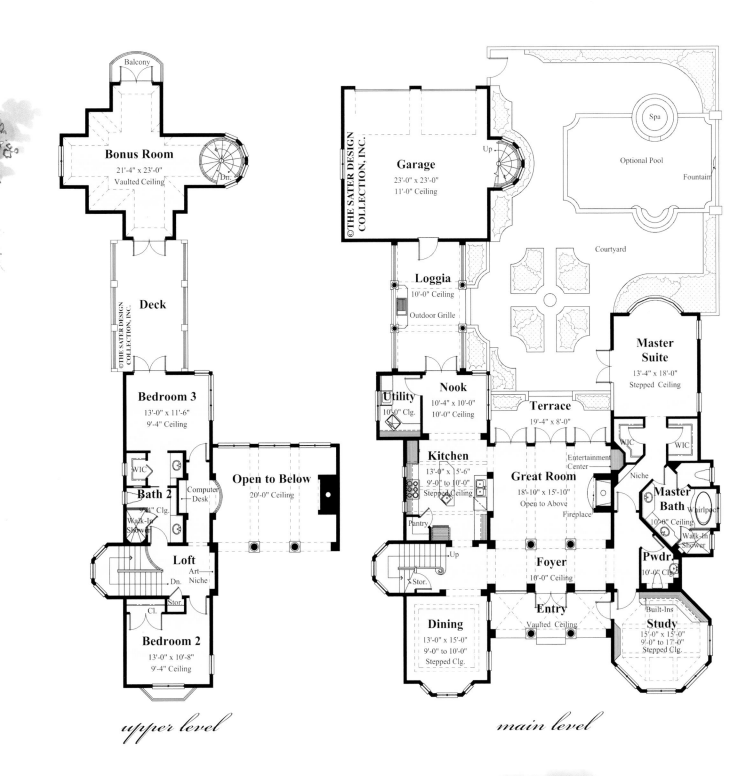

Bonus Room
21'-4" x 23'-0"
Vaulted Ceiling

Balcony

Dn.

Deck

Bedroom 3
13'-0" x 11'-6"
9'-4" Ceiling

WIC

Computer Desk

Open to Below
20'-0" Ceiling

Bath 2
7'-4" Clg.
Walk-In Shower

Loft
Art Niche
Dn.
Stor.
Cl.

Bedroom 2
13'-0" x 10'-8"
9'-4" Ceiling

upper level

© THE SATER DESIGN COLLECTION, INC.

Garage
23'-0" x 23'-0"
11'-0" Ceiling

Up

Spa

Optional Pool

Fountain

Courtyard

Loggia
10'-0" Ceiling

Outdoor Grille

Master Suite
13'-4" x 18'-0"
Stepped Ceiling

Utility
10'-0" Clg.

Nook
10'-4" x 10'-0"
10'-0" Ceiling

Terrace
19'-4" x 8'-0"

WIC

WIC

Kitchen
13'-0" x 5'-6"
9'-0" to 10'-0"
Stepped Ceiling

Entertainment Center

Great Room
18'-10" x 15'-10"
Open to Above
Fireplace

Niche

Master Bath
10'-0" Ceiling
Whirlpool
Walk-In Shower

Pantry

Foyer
10'-0" Ceiling

Pwdr.
10'-0" Clg.

Up

Stor.

Dining
13'-0" x 15'-0"
9'-0" to 10'-0"
Stepped Clg.

Entry
Vaulted Ceiling

Built-Ins

Study
15'-0" x 15'-0"
9'-0" to 17'-0"
Stepped Clg.

main level

© The Sater Design Collection, Inc.

rear elevation

www.saterdesign.com

© The Sater Design Collection, Inc.

© The Sater Design Collection, Inc.

Vasari

ROME BEAUTY — *Cut-stone masonry highlights creamy-white stucco evocative of the picturesque Renaissance seaside villas of the Italian coast.*

Sculpted window heads and spiral pilasters set off an impressive stone arch and carved columns, creating a Propylaeum-style entry with this cutting-edge yet deeply comfortable villa. An uninhibited spirit prevails within—a gallery foyer and loft deepens the central living/dining room, allowing a stepped ceiling to soar above open vistas defined only by decorative columns. A two-sided fireplace warms the central area as well as a spacious study that boasts built-ins and a private porch. Above the entry, a sun porch with a barrel ceiling and a fanlight transom permits sunlight or moonlight to invigorate the loft—an inviting space that connects the family's sleeping quarters with a suite designed for a teenager or live-in guest. The main level brags a cabana-style guest suite, with access to a compartmented bath and shower from the veranda.

PLAN | *8025*

Bedroom: 5   Width: 58'0"

Bath: 5-1/2   Depth: 65'0"

Foundation: Slab or
  optional basement

Exterior Walls: 2x6

Main Level: 1,995 sq ft

Upper Level: 2,165 sq ft

Living Area: 4,160 sq ft

Price Code: **L2**

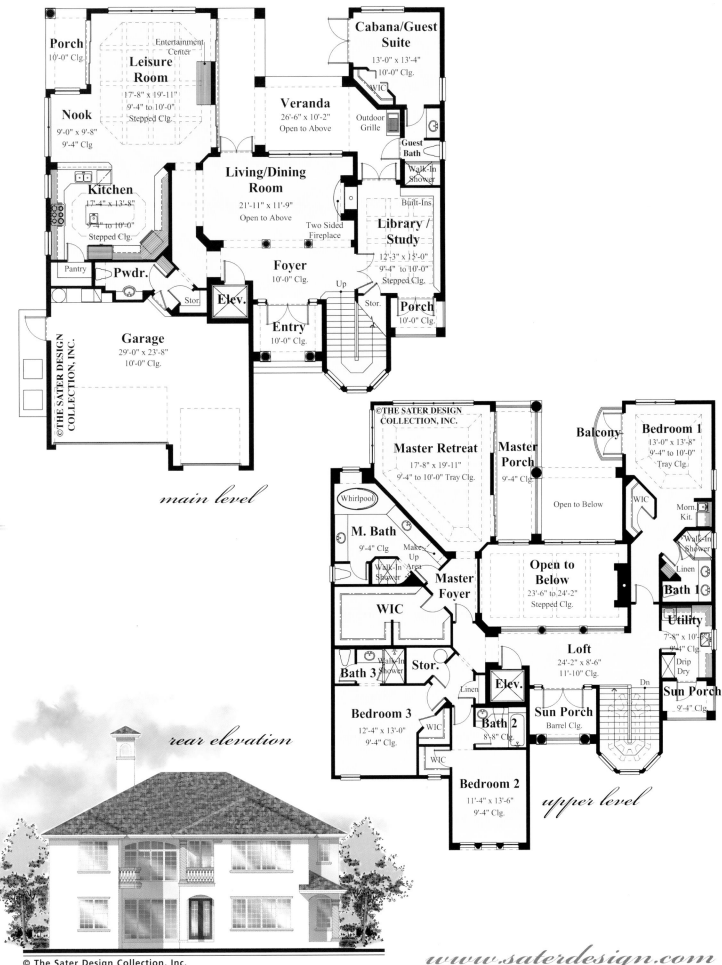

Porch
10'-0" Clg.

Leisure Room
17'-8" x 19'-11"
9'-4" to 10'-0"
Stepped Clg.

Entertainment Center

Cabana/Guest Suite
13'-0" x 13'-4"
10'-0" Clg.

WIC

Nook
9'-0" x 9'-8"
9'-4" Clg.

Veranda
26'-6" x 10'-2"
Open to Above

Outdoor Grille

Guest Bath

Walk-In Shower

Kitchen
17'-4" x 13'-8"
9'-4" to 10'-0"
Stepped Clg.

Living/Dining Room
21'-11" x 11'-9"
Open to Above

Built-Ins

Library / Study
12'-3" x 15'-0"
9'-4" to 10'-0"
Stepped Clg.

Two Sided Fireplace

Foyer
10'-0" Clg.

Pantry

Pwdr.

Stor.

Elev.

Up

Stor.

Porch
10'-0" Clg.

©THE SATER DESIGN COLLECTION, INC.

Garage
29'-0" x 23'-8"
10'-0" Clg.

Entry
10'-0" Clg.

main level

©THE SATER DESIGN COLLECTION, INC.

Master Retreat
17'-8" x 19'-11"
9'-4" to 10'-0" Tray Clg.

Master Porch
9'-4" Clg.

Balcony

Bedroom 1
13'-0" x 13'-8"
9'-4" to 10'-0"
Tray Clg.

Whirlpool

M. Bath
9'-4" Clg.

Make Up Area

Open to Below

WIC

Morn. Kit.

Walk-In Shower

Walk-In Shower

Linen

Bath 1

Master Foyer

Open to Below
23'-6" to 24'-2"
Stepped Clg.

WIC

Utility
7'-8" x 10'-0"
9'-4" Clg.

Drip Dry

Bath 3

Walk-In Shower

Stor.

Elev.

Linen

Loft
24'-2" x 8'-6"
11'-10" Clg.

Dn

Sun Porch
9'-4" Clg.

Bedroom 3
12'-4" x 13'-0"
9'-4" Clg.

WIC

Bath 2
8'-8" Clg.

Sun Porch
Barrel Clg.

WIC

Bedroom 2
11'-4" x 13'-6"
9'-4" Clg.

upper level

rear elevation

© The Sater Design Collection, Inc.

© The Sater Design Collection, Inc.

Mercato

SUN COUNTRY — *Soak up the scenery and a wealth of sunlight through hosts of French doors in the great room—a great place to kick off the shoes or put on a party.*

Spiral columns articulate an elegant arcade that's merely the beginning of this Mediterranean villa. Inside, a beamed ceiling contributes a sense of spaciousness to the heart of the home, while walls of glass draw the outdoors inside. A repertoire of palazzo-sur-mer forms satisfies a singular architectural theme: varied ceiling treatments and sculpted arches define the wide-open interior, permitting flexibility as well as great views. The great room is anchored by a massive fireplace flanked by built-in shelves and an entertainment center—visible from the kitchen via a pass-through. A private foyer in the master wing links the owners' bedroom and dressing space with a sensational bath that boasts a whirlpool tub and a walk-in shower. Plenty of windows brighten this suite, which provides separate access to the veranda.

PLAN | *8028*

Bedroom: 3   Width: 62'10"
Bath: 2-1/2   Depth: 73'6"
Foundation: Slab or
  optional basement
Exterior Walls: 2x6

Main Level: 2,191 sq ft

Living Area: 2,191 sq ft

Price Code: **C2**

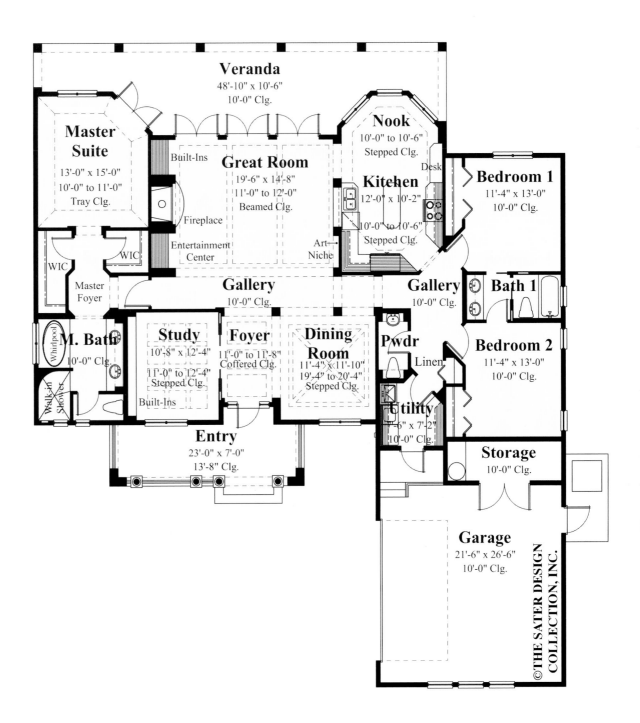

Veranda
48'-10" x 10'-6"
10'-0" Clg.

Master Suite
13'-0" x 15'-0"
10'-0" to 11'-0"
Tray Clg.

Built-Ins

Great Room
19'-6" x 14'-8"
11'-0" to 12'-0"
Beamed Clg.

Nook
10'-0" to 10'-6"
Stepped Clg.

Desk

Bedroom 1
11'-4" x 13'-0"
10'-0" Clg.

Kitchen
12'-0" x 10'-2"
10'-0" to 10'-6"
Stepped Clg.

Fireplace

Entertainment Center

Art Niche

WIC

WIC

Master Foyer

Gallery
10'-0" Clg.

Gallery
10'-0" Clg.

Bath 1

M. Bath
10'-0" Clg.

Whirlpool

Study
10'-8" x 12'-4"
11'-0" to 12'-4"
Stepped Clg.
Built-Ins

Foyer
11'-0" to 11'-8"
Coffered Clg.

Dining Room
11'-4" x 11'-10"
19'-4" to 20'-4"
Stepped Clg.

Pwdr

Linen

Bedroom 2
11'-4" x 13'-0"
10'-0" Clg.

Walk-in Shower

Utility
-6" x 7'-2"
10'-0" Clg.

Entry
23'-0" x 7'-0"
13'-8" Clg.

Storage
10'-0" Clg.

Garage
21'-6" x 26'-6"
10'-0" Clg.

©THE SATER DESIGN COLLECTION, INC.

rear elevation

© The Sater Design Collection, Inc.

Isabella

BOCA ROCOCO — *Decorative masonry lends 18th-century panache to a triplet of pediments—a mix that offers just the right historic splash to a New World villa.*

Rococo elements frame an elaborate double portico, lending contrast to rugged stone accents and a rusticated stucco facade. A symmetrical arrangement of fanlights and tall windows plays counterpoint to varying rooflines and contemporary twists to classic lines. Smooth stucco walls inspire an authentic feel throughout the interior, warming the wide-open spaces. The paneled entry leads to a two-story foyer that opens to the formal rooms, defined by arches and columns. To the front of the plan, a secluded study or library boasts access to a private portico. Private zones frame the rear loggias—a spacious guest suite, with a cabana bath, and the casual living area both open to outdoor spaces. On the upper level, a dramatic balcony loft overlooks the living room and leads to a sun porch. To the right, a private foyer introduces the spectacular master suite—a luxury retreat with a garden bath and a sun porch off the bedroom.

PLAN | *8033*

Bedroom: 5   Width: 58'0"

Bath: 5-1/2   Depth: 65'0"

Foundation: Slab or optional basement

Exterior Walls: 2x6

Main Level: 2,163 sq ft

Upper Level: 2,302 sq ft

Living Area: 4,465 sq ft

Price Code: **L2**

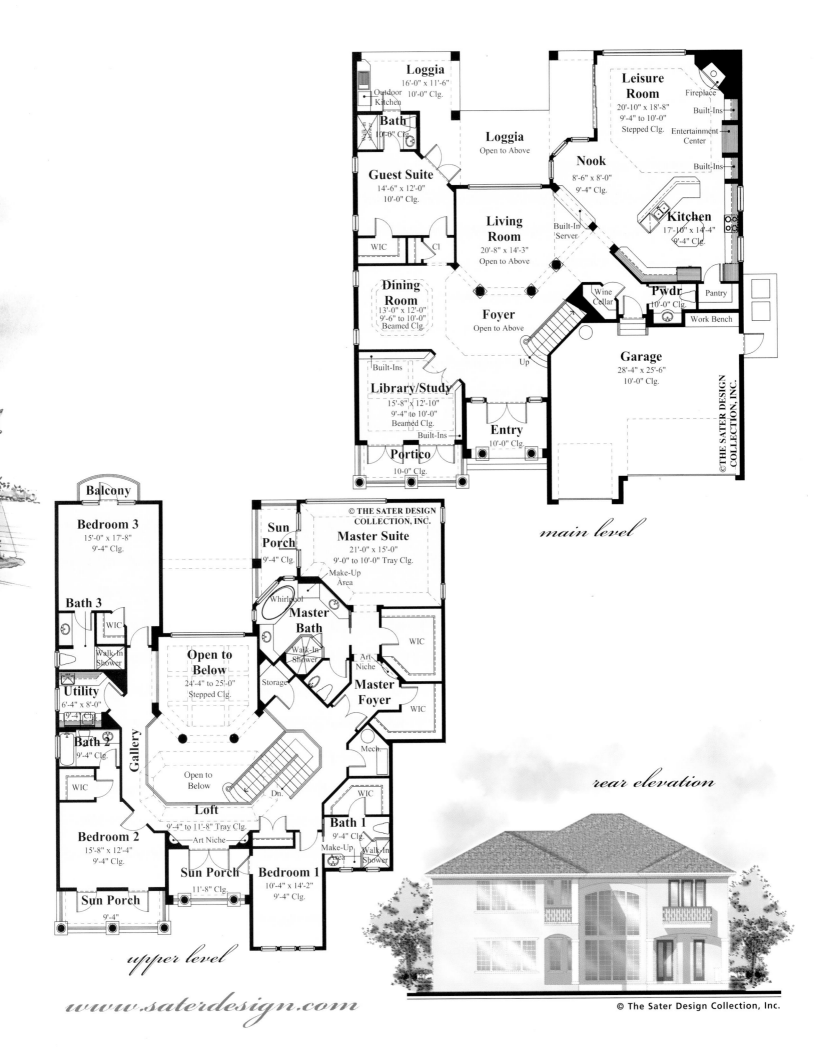

© The Sater Design Collection, Inc.

Laparelli

RETRO COOL — *Palladian influences create an out-of-this-world inside/outside home that captures seaside breezes and a bit of the past.*

Romantic elements reside throughout this Italian villa, melding high style and great views with a profound level of comfort. Massive arches, stepped ceilings and French doors embrace ancient Mediterranean lines, creating a perfect forum for both entertaining and repose. A breezy lanai wraps the rear elevation, inviting fresh air to mingle. Arch-topped windows bring natural light into the forward formal spaces, while retreating walls on the lanai side extend both public and private realms beyond the home's footprint. Well-organized and equipped for sophisticated gatherings, the kitchen serves the formal dining room via a servery and gallery, while a wet bar and cabana bath announce the casual living space. The owners' retreat provides a magnificent bedroom with a sitting bay, morning kitchen and private access to the wraparound lanai. A dressing area framed by room-sized walk-in closets leads to a spacious bath with garden views.

PLAN | *8035*

Bedroom: 3   Width: 83'10"
Bath: 4   Depth: 106'0"
Foundation: Slab
Exterior Walls: 2x6

Main Level: 3,942 sq ft

Living Area: 3,942 sq ft

Price Code: **L1**

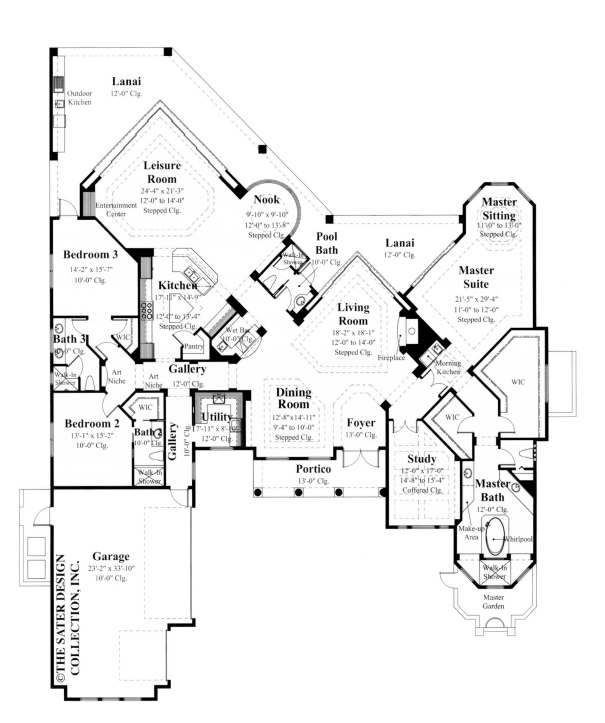

Lanai
12'-0" Clg.

Outdoor Kitchen

Leisure Room
24'-4" x 21'-3"
12'-0" to 14'-0"
Stepped Clg.

Nook
9'-10" x 9'-10"
12'-0" to 13'-8"
Stepped Clg.

Master Sitting
11'-0" to 13'-0"
Stepped Clg.

Pool Bath
10'-0" Clg.

Lanai
12'-0" Clg.

Bedroom 3
14'-2" x 15'-7"
10'-0" Clg.

Walk-In Shower

Master Suite
21'-5" x 29'-4"
11'-0" to 12'-0"
Stepped Clg.

Entertainment Center

Kitchen
17'-11" x 14'-9"
12'-0" to 13'-4"
Stepped Clg.

Living Room
18'-2" x 18'-1"
12'-0" to 14'-0"
Stepped Clg.

Wet Bar
10'-0" Clg.

Bath 3
10'-0" Clg.

WIC

Pantry

Fireplace

Morning Kitchen

WIC

Walk-In Shower

Art Niche

Art Niche

Gallery
12'-0" Clg.

Bedroom 2
13'-1" x 15'-2"
10'-0" Clg.

WIC

Bath 2
10'-0" Clg.

Gallery
10'-0" Clg.

Utility
17'-11" x 8'-0"
12'-0" Clg.

Dining Room
12'-8" x 14'-11"
9'-4" to 10'-0"
Stepped Clg.

Foyer
13'-0" Clg.

WIC

Study
12'-0" x 17'-0"
14'-8" to 15'-4"
Coffered Clg.

Master Bath
12'-0" Clg.

Walk-In Shower

Make-up Area

Whirlpool

Portico
13'-0" Clg.

Garage
23'-2" x 33'-10"
10'-0" Clg.

Master Garden

©THE SATER DESIGN COLLECTION, INC.

rear elevation

Raphaello

JOIE D'VIVRE — *Glass towers and Palladian windows establish an Italian Country theme that's entirely at home with this manor's innovative character.*

Arched windows and barrel-tiled roofs set off smooth, cast-stone elements with this splendid villa. The rich saturated hues of the terra facade enliven the streetscape and link the design to its European roots. Turrets integrate the layered elevation, which draws its inspiration from 16th-century forms, with symmetry, brackets and pilasters. New-world allocations of space defy tradition throughout the interior, creating an avant-garde spirit and easing everyday functions. Living spaces oriented to the rear of the plan take in views and natural light through great walls of glass that also grant access to the lanai. Open arrangements of space are partially defined by varying ceiling treatments throughout the home— and lend texture and flow to the interior. On the upper level, secondary bedrooms adjoin a compartmented bath and open to a shared deck. A computer loft leads to a spacious bonus room—a perfect place for guest quarters.

PLAN	*8037*

Bedroom: 3   Width: 72'0"

Bath: 3-1/2   Depth: 68'3"

Foundation: Slab or
    optional basement

Exterior Walls: 2x6

Main Level: 2,250 sq ft

Upper Level: 663 sq ft

Living Area: 2,913 sq ft

Bonus Room: 351 sq ft

Price Code: **C3**

Lanai
26'-0" x 15'-10"
10'-0" Clg.

**Master
Suite**
13'-2" x 21'-2"
12'-0" to 13'-0"
Stepped Clg.

Walk-In
Shower

Bath 1
10'-0" Clg.

L

Great Room
21'-3" x 17'-8"
Vaulted w/
Beamed Clg.

Fireplace

Entertainment
Center

Built-In
Shelves

Nook
9'-0" to 10'-0"
Stepped Clg.

Kitchen
13'-0" x 13'-9"
9'-0" to 9'-6"
Stepped Clg.

**Dining
Room**
11'-0" x 12'-8"
9'-0" to 10'-0"
Coffered Clg.

WIC

WIC

Walk-In
Shower

**Master
Bath**
12'-0" Clg.

Whirlpool

Study
11'-0" x 15'-4"
16'-4" to 17'-4"
Beamed Clg.

Foyer
18'-8" to 19'-8"
Stepped Clg.

Dn.

Storage

Gallery
10'-0" Clg.

Utility
6'-8" x 12'-0"
10'-0" Clg.

Pwdr.
10'-0" Clg.

Entry
18'-8" Clg.

main level

Garage
21'-0" x 25'-4"
10'-0" Clg.

©THE SATER DESIGN COLLECTION, INC.

Deck
26'-0" x 15'-10"

©**THE SATER DESIGN
COLLECTION, INC.**

Bedroom 1
13'-0" x 14'-6"
9'-4" to 10'-4"
Tray Clg.

Bedroom 2
12'-2" x 14'-4"
10'-0" Clg.

Bath 2
10'-0" Clg.

WIC

Walk-In
Shower

Linen

Loft 10'-0"

Dn.

Desk

Clg.

Niche

**Bonus
Bath**
9'-8" Clg.

Walk-In
Shower

upper level

**Bonus
Room**
16'-6" x 19'-2"
Vaulted to
9'-8" Clg.

rear elevation

www.saterdesign.com

© The Sater Design Collection, Inc.

Bellini

VILLA GRANDE — *Arches, columns and an enchanting series of decorative brackets define the perfect blend of old and new—and conceal an open interior layered with details.*

Classic architectural lines surround an entry portico inspired by original Italian villas. Ancient and modern elements come together throughout the interior, juxtaposing rusticated beamed ceilings with up-to-the-minute electronics. An open gallery and a sculpted arcade announce the living/dining room—a splendid space anchored by a massive fireplace. French doors invite the outdoors inside, where fresh breezes mingle with an authentic European temperament. Contemporary spaces reside in the private realm: a state-of-the-art kitchen overlooks a bumped-out morning nook and a media room with retreating walls. A wraparound veranda brags oceans of space for enjoying the great scenery, plus an outdoor grille and a secluded area for meals alfresco. The owners' wing includes a private study—which could easily convert to a guest room—and a gallery hall that leads to a rambling retreat with a walk-in shower and a whirlpool tub.

PLAN | *8042*

Bedroom: 3   Width: 84'0"

Bath: 2 Full   Depth: 92'2"
       2 Half

Foundation: Slab

Exterior Walls: 2x6

Main Level: 3,351 sq ft

Living Area: 3,351 sq ft

Price Code: **C4**

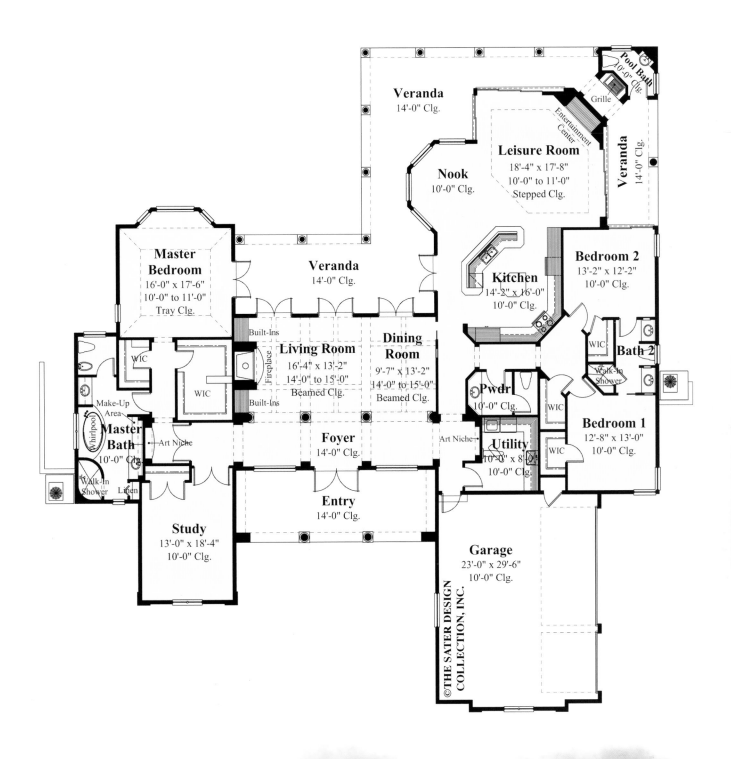

Veranda
14'-0" Clg.

Pool Bath
10'-0" Clg.

Grille

Entertainment Center

Leisure Room
18'-4" x 17'-8"
10'-0" to 11'-0"
Stepped Clg.

Veranda
14'-0" Clg.

Nook
10'-0" Clg.

Master Bedroom
16'-0" x 17'-6"
10'-0" to 11'-0"
Tray Clg.

Veranda
14'-0" Clg.

Kitchen
14'-2" x 16'-0"
10'-0" Clg.

Bedroom 2
13'-2" x 12'-2"
10'-0" Clg.

Built-Ins

WIC

WIC

Living Room
16'-4" x 13'-2"
14'-0" to 15'-0"
Beamed Clg.

Dining Room
9'-7" x 13'-2"
14'-0" to 15'-0"
Beamed Clg.

Fireplace

WIC

Bath 2

Walk-In Shower

Built-Ins

Pwdr
10'-0" Clg.

WIC

Make-Up Area

Master Bath
10'-0" Clg.

Whirlpool

Art Niche

Foyer
14'-0" Clg.

Art Niche

Utility
10'-0" x 8'
10'-0" Clg.

Bedroom 1
12'-8" x 13'-0"
10'-0" Clg.

WIC

Walk-In Shower

Linen

Entry
14'-0" Clg.

Study
13'-0" x 18'-4"
10'-0" Clg.

Garage
23'-0" x 29'-6"
10'-0" Clg.

©THE SATER DESIGN COLLECTION, INC.

rear elevation

© The Sater Design Collection, Inc.

Salina

WORLD CLASS — *A highly sculpted elevation achieves its authentic flavor with an elaborate display of masonry, clean lines and plenty of windows.*

Hipped rooflines and carved eave brackets evoke a sense of the past, yet also step into the future with a footprint that's designed for 21st-century lifestyles. An engaging blend of old and new prevails inside: beamed and coffered ceilings play counterpoint to into-the-future amenities—a wet bar that serves private and public zones, cutting-edge culinary appliances in the gourmet kitchen, and a stand-alone media center between the leisure and game rooms. Varied volumes and gently rounded arches define the easy transitions between well-appointed rooms and open spaces. A private vestibule links the master retreat with a study rich with wood. Secluded to the rear of the plan, guest quarters include a cabana-style bath that opens to a separate veranda—also accessed from the leisure room—with an outdoor grille and plenty of space for dining alfresco.

PLAN | *8043*

Bedroom: 4   Width: 80'0"
Bath: 3-1/2   Depth: 104'8"
Foundation: Slab or
    optional basement
Exterior Walls: 2x6

Main Level: 3,743 sq ft

Living Area: 3,743 sq ft

Price Code: **L1**

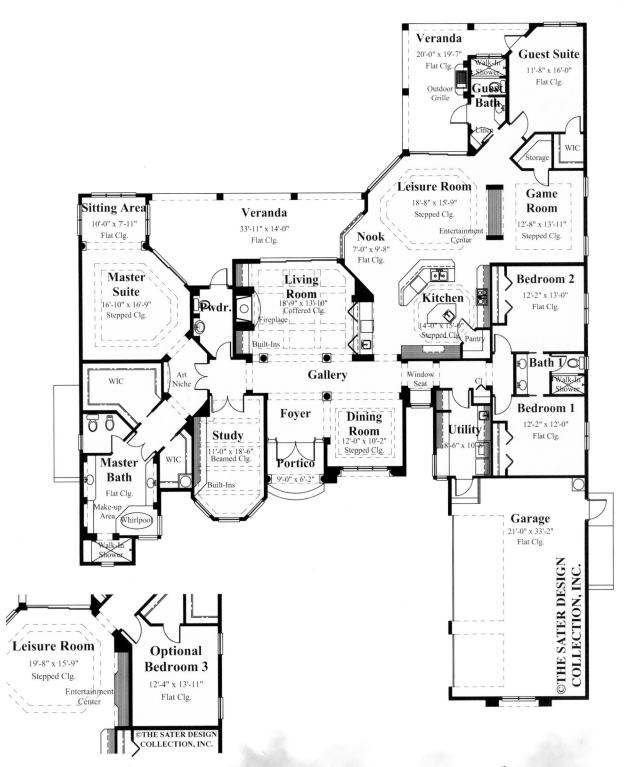

Veranda
20'-0" x 19'-7"
Flat Clg.

Outdoor Grille

Guest Bath

Walk-In Shower

Guest Suite
11'-8" x 16'-0"
Flat Clg.

Linen

WIC

Storage

Sitting Area
10'-0" x 7'-11"
Flat Clg.

Veranda
33'-11" x 14'-0"
Flat Clg.

Leisure Room
18'-8" x 15'-9"
Stepped Clg.

Entertainment Center

Game Room
12'-8" x 13'-11"
Stepped Clg.

Master Suite
16'-10" x 16'-9"
Stepped Clg.

Pwdr.

Living Room
18'-9" x 13'-10"
Coffered Clg.

Fireplace

Built-Ins

Nook
7'-0" x 9'-8"
Flat Clg.

Kitchen
14'-0" x 15'-0"
Stepped Clg.

Pantry

Bedroom 2
12'-2" x 13'-0"
Flat Clg.

WIC

Art Niche

Gallery

Window Seat

Cl

Bath 1

Walk-In Shower

Foyer

Study
11'-0" x 18'-6"
Beamed Clg.

Built-Ins

WIC

Dining Room
12'-0" x 10'-2"
Stepped Clg.

Utility
8'-6" x 10'

Bedroom 1
12'-2" x 12'-0"
Flat Clg.

Master Bath
Flat Clg.

Portico
9'-0" x 6'-2"

Make-up Area

Whirlpool

Walk-In Shower

Garage
21'-0" x 33'-2"
Flat Clg.

©THE SATER DESIGN COLLECTION, INC.

Leisure Room
19'-8" x 15'-9"
Stepped Clg.

Entertainment Center

Optional Bedroom 3
12'-4" x 13'-11"
Flat Clg.

©THE SATER DESIGN COLLECTION, INC.

rear elevation

www.saterdesign.com

© The Sater Design Collection, Inc.

Corsini

CASA D' ORO — *Ancient lines converge with smart, tomorrow-house function in an Italian eclectic design that simmers with seaside sensibilities.*

Corbels, columns and shapely carved balusters rooted in a timeless vocabulary step into the future with this grand villa. Triplets of French doors deck out the facade, adding light to the front of the home and establishing a striking street presence. The central gallery opens to the heart of the home, an outside-in space that brings in breezes and light and offers a link to nature. A lateral arrangement of the kitchen, loggia, morning nook and formal dining room eases the service of meals, from planned events with hors d'oeuvres alfresco to grilling parties by the pool. To the right of the plan, the owners' wing includes a forward study and a powder bath—designed to flex from a private retreat to guest quarters or even a nursery. The upper level provides a gallery loft that grants interior vistas through the great room, and connects four secondary bedrooms—one with a private deck-that share two baths.

PLAN	*8049*

Bedroom: 5	Width: 71'0"
Bath: 3-1/2	Depth: 72'0"
Foundation: Slab	
Exterior Walls: 2x6	

Main Level:	2,163 sq ft
Upper Level:	1,415 sq ft

Living Area: 3,578 sq ft

Price Code: **L1**

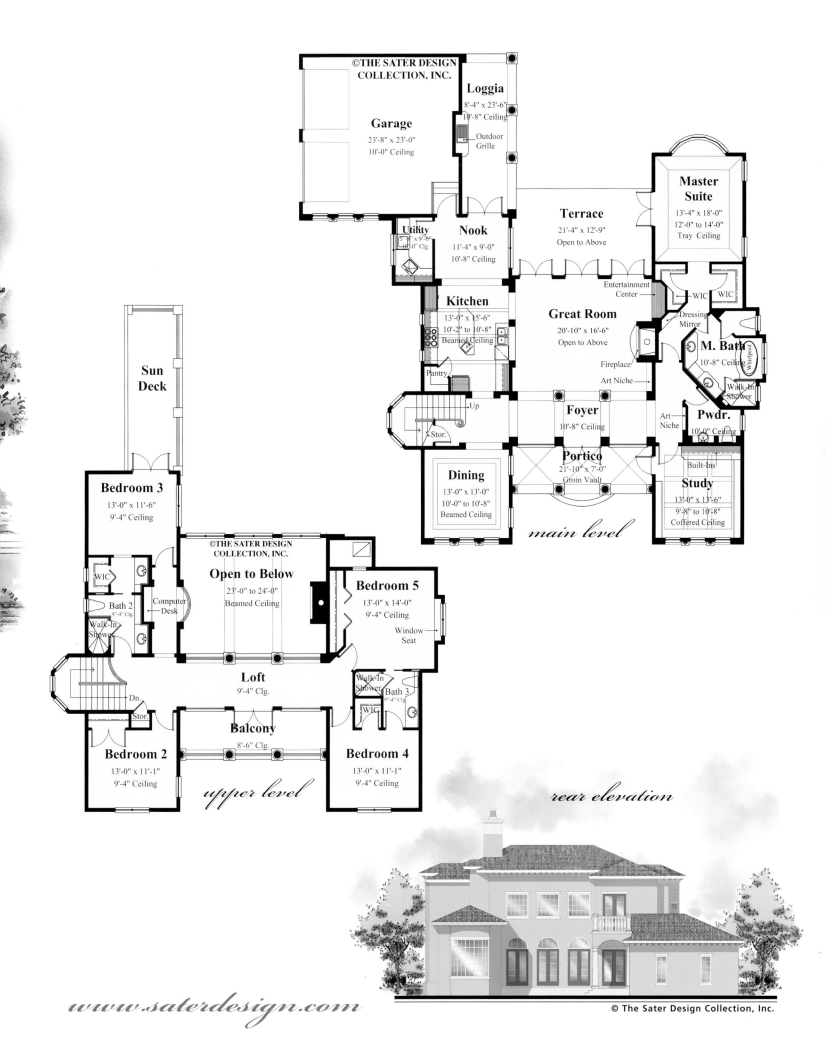

©THE SATER DESIGN
COLLECTION, INC.

Garage
23'-8" x 23'-0"
10'-0" Ceiling

Loggia
8'-4" x 23'-6"
10'-8" Ceiling

Outdoor Grille

Terrace
21'-4" x 12'-9"
Open to Above

Master Suite
13'-4" x 18'-0"
12'-0" to 14'-0"
Tray Ceiling

Utility
5'-8" x 9'-6"
10'-0" Clg.

Nook
11'-4" x 9'-0"
10'-8" Ceiling

Entertainment Center

WIC   WIC

Kitchen
13'-0" x 15'-6"
10'-2" to 10'-8"
Beamed Ceiling

Great Room
20'-10" x 16'-6"
Open to Above

Dressing Mirror

M. Bath
10'-8" Ceiling

Whirlpool

Pantry

Fireplace

Art Niche

Walk-In Shower

Foyer
10'-8" Ceiling

Art Niche

Pwdr.
10'-0" Ceiling

Up   Stor.

Dining
13'-0" x 13'-0"
10'-0" to 10'-8"
Beamed Ceiling

Portico
21'-10" x 7'-0"
Groin Vault

Built-Ins

Study
13'-0" x 13'-6"
9'-8" to 10'-8"
Coffered Ceiling

main level

Sun Deck

Bedroom 3
13'-0" x 11'-6"
9'-4" Ceiling

WIC

Bath 2
9'-4" Clg.

Computer Desk

Walk-In Shower

©THE SATER DESIGN
COLLECTION, INC.

Open to Below
23'-0" to 24'-0"
Beamed Ceiling

Bedroom 5
13'-0" x 14'-0"
9'-4" Ceiling

Window Seat

Loft
9'-4" Clg.

Dn.   Stor.

Walk-In Shower

Bath 3

WIC

Balcony
8'-6" Clg.

Bedroom 2
13'-0" x 11'-1"
9'-4" Ceiling

upper level

Bedroom 4
13'-0" x 11'-1"
9'-4" Ceiling

rear elevation

www.saterdesign.com

© The Sater Design Collection, Inc.

Massimo

OUTSIDE-IN — *Colonial lines evoke the ancient forms of the houses of Tuscany, yet this grand manor steps boldly into the present.*

Sun-splashed stucco walls set off by rows of windows take on a sense of whimsy with a stacked-stone turret and varied rooflines. A breezy portico shelters the entry from heat and sun, while the colonnade recalls the beauty of classic Roman arches. A side courtyard complements a veranda that wraps around the rear of the plan, bordered by walls of glass and bay windows. Four sets of French doors open the central living and dining space to the world outside—or just set the table on the lanai for open air meals. The private realm includes a main-level flex room with an adjoining bath and optional space for cabinetry or a wardrobe. Upstairs, Bedrooms 1 and 2 open to a shared deck with rear-property views. A loft with a balcony overlook provides plenty of space for books and computers.

PLAN | 8057

Bedroom: 5   Width: 69'4"

Bath: 4-1/2   Depth: 95'4"

Foundation: Slab or
    optional basement

Exterior Walls: 2x6

Main Level: 2,920 sq ft

Upper Level: 1,478 sq ft

Living Area: 4,398 sq ft

Price Code: **L2**

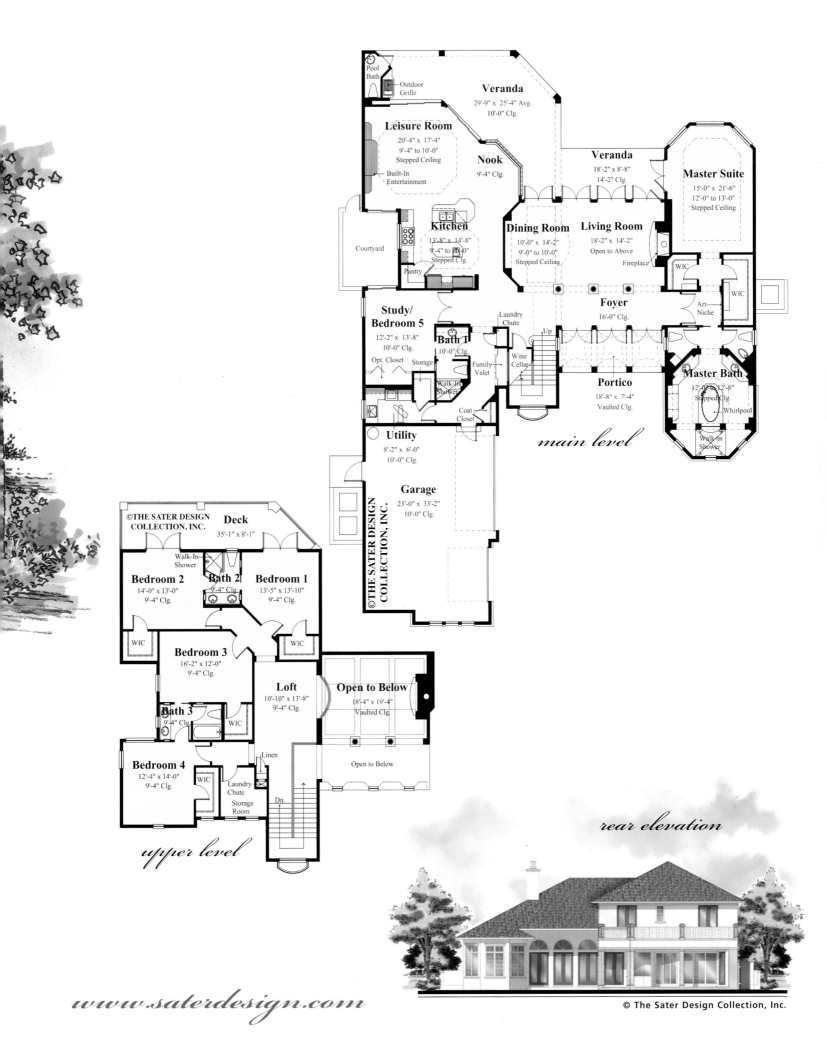

Pool Bath

Outdoor Grille

Veranda
29'-9" x 25'-4" Avg.
10'-0" Clg.

Leisure Room
20'-4" x 17'-4"
9'-4" to 10'-0"
Stepped Ceiling

Built-In Entertainment

Nook
9'-4" Clg.

Veranda
18'-2" x 8'-8"
14'-2" Clg.

Master Suite
15'-0" x 21'-6"
12'-0" to 13'-0"
Stepped Ceiling

Kitchen
13'-8" x 14'-8"
9'-4" to 10'-0"
Stepped Clg.

Dining Room
10'-0" x 14'-2"
9'-0" to 10'-0"
Stepped Ceiling

Living Room
18'-2" x 14'-2"
Open to Above

Courtyard

Pantry

Fireplace

WIC

WIC

Study/Bedroom 5
12'-2" x 13'-8"
10'-0" Clg.

Bath 1
10'-0" Clg.

Laundry Chute

Foyer
16'-0" Clg.

Art Niche

Opt. Closet

Storage

Walk-In Shower

Family Valet

Wine Cellar

Up

Portico
18'-8" x 7'-4"
Vaulted Clg.

Master Bath
12'-0" to 12'-8"
Stepped Clg.

Whirlpool

Coat Closet

Walk-In Shower

Utility
8'-2" x 6'-0"
10'-0" Clg.

main level

Garage
23'-0" x 33'-2"
10'-0" Clg.

©THE SATER DESIGN COLLECTION, INC.

Deck
35'-1" x 8'-1"

©THE SATER DESIGN COLLECTION, INC.

Walk-In Shower

Bedroom 2
14'-0" x 13'-0"
9'-4" Clg.

Bath 2
9'-4" Clg.

Bedroom 1
13'-5" x 13'-10"
9'-4" Clg.

WIC

WIC

Bedroom 3
16'-2" x 12'-0"
9'-4" Clg.

Loft
10'-10" x 13'-8"
9'-4" Clg.

Open to Below
18'-4" x 19'-4"
Vaulted Clg.

Bath 3
9'-4" Clg.

WIC

Linen

Open to Below

Bedroom 4
12'-4" x 14'-0"
9'-4" Clg.

WIC

Laundry Chute

Storage Room

Dn.

upper level

rear elevation

www.saterdesign.com

© The Sater Design Collection, Inc.

© The Sater Design Collection, Inc.

Simone

TERRA FIRMA — *With the charm of a rustic cottage planted in the hills of Tuscany, this great estate offers room to ramble and more than just a taste of the outdoors.*

Stacked stone gables dramatically define the neighborhood presence of this Italian villa. Fanlights, carved balusters and square transoms enrich the sculpted elevation, and quietly evoke the past. Beyond the entry, the plan offers well-defined rooms and wide-open spaces, with views of nature everywhere. A private vestibule just off the foyer leads to a powder bath and an elegant study that overlooks the front property. Tapered columns define the open boundaries of the formal dining room, permitting interior vistas as well as easy service from the gourmet kitchen. A guest suite adjoins the leisure room, providing a pocket door for privacy, and its own access to the lanai. The owners' retreat opens to an outdoor area that includes an optional grille and cabinets—for alfresco dining. Separate vanity and wardrobe spaces highlight the master suite. A family valet, conveniently located, provides the perfect place to drop your keys and packages.

PLAN | *8059*

Bedroom: 4   Width: 67'0"

Bath: 3-1/2   Depth: 91'8"

Foundation: Slab

Exterior Walls: 8"CBS or 2x6

Main Level: 3,231 sq ft

Living Area: 3,231 sq ft

Price Code: **C4**

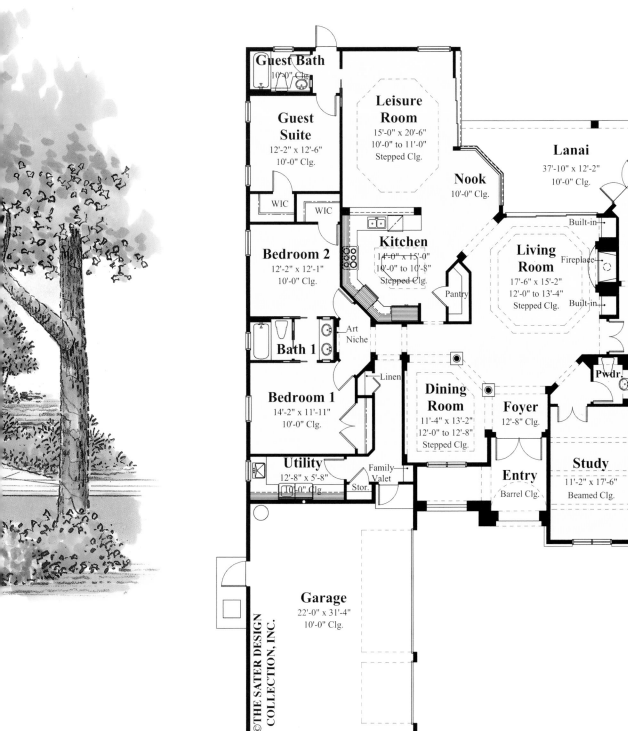

Guest Bath
10'-0" Clg.

Guest Suite
12'-2" x 12'-6"
10'-0" Clg.

Leisure Room
15'-0" x 20'-6"
10'-0" to 11'-0"
Stepped Clg.

Lanai
37'-10" x 12'-2"
10'-0" Clg.

Grille

Nook
10'-0" Clg.

Master Suite
15'-10" x 15'-2"
10'-0" to 11'-0"
Stepped Clg.

WIC

WIC

Built-in

Bedroom 2
12'-2" x 12'-1"
10'-0" Clg.

Kitchen
14'-0" x 15'-0"
10'-0" to 10'-8"
Stepped Clg.

Living Room
17'-6" x 15'-2"
12'-0" to 13'-4"
Stepped Clg.

Fireplace

WIC

Pantry

Built-in

Art Niche

Bath 1

Linen

Linen

Pwdr.

Master Bath
9'-4" to 10'-0"
Stepped Clg.

Privacy Garden

Whirlpool

Bedroom 1
14'-2" x 11'-11"
10'-0" Clg.

Dining Room
11'-4" x 13'-2"
12'-0" to 12'-8"
Stepped Clg.

Foyer
12'-8" Clg.

Walk-In Shower

Dressing Area

Utility
12'-8" x 5'-8"
10'-0" Clg.

Family Valet

Stor.

Entry
Barrel Clg.

Study
11'-2" x 17'-6"
Beamed Clg.

Garage
22'-0" x 31'-4"
10'-0" Clg.

©THE SATER DESIGN COLLECTION, INC.

rear elevation

© The Sater Design Collection, Inc.

Santa Trinita

STYLE WITH SUBSTANCE — *Rough stone, framed by smooth stucco, announces a 21st-century plan of well-defined spaces and wide-open views.*

Tuscan charm invites a feeling of home outside and in, with floor-to-ceiling windows to let in the sun. A recessed masonry entry echoes the shape of the stately turrets, and provides both shade and shelter, easing the transition to the indoors. Designated as the public zone, the front of the home features an arrangement of formal spaces intended for dining and entertaining. With richly textured amenities such as a stone mantel, highly crafted cabinetry and stepped ceilings, the well-appointed rooms offer a chic arena for formal or casual gatherings. To the rear of the plan, the leisure room opens from the kitchen, which is geared for crowd-sized events or family movie nights. A gallery hall runs the width of the plan, linking a cluster of secondary bedrooms with the master suite. A family valet, conveniently located, provides the perfect place to drop your keys and packages.

PLAN | *8063*

Bedroom: 4   Width: 68'8"
Bath: 3-1/2   Depth: 91'8"
Foundation: Slab
Exterior Walls: 2x6

Main Level: 3,497 sq ft

Living Area: 3,497sq ft

Price Code: **C4**

Sitting Area
9'-8" x 7'-6"
10'-0" Clg.

Lanai
25'-0" x 14'-0"
10'-0" Clg.

Living Room
18'-2" x 22'-8"
10'-0" to 11'-4"
Stepped Clg.

Guest Bath

Linen

Guest Suite
13'-0" x 13'-0"
10'-0" Clg.

Master Suite
13'-8" x 17'-3"
10'-0" to 11'-0"
Stepped Clg.

Nook
10'-0" Clg.

Built-Ins

Pwdr
10'-0" Clg

Living Room
16'-8" x 16'-6"
12'-0" to 13'-4"
Stepped Clg.

Fireplace

Built-Ins

Kitchen
15'-4" x 15'-4"
10'-0" to 11'-0"
Stepped Clg.

Pantry

WIC   WIC

Bedroom 2
13'-0" x 12'-8"
10'-0" Clg.

Bath 1
10'-0" Clg.

WIC

M. Foyer
10'-0" Clg.

Linen

Family Valet

Foyer
13'-4" Clg.

Study
11'-4" x 14'-2"
13'-0" to 14'-4"
Stepped Clg.

Dining Room
11'-4" x 13'-6"
14'-0" to 15'-4"
Stepped Clg.

Linen

Bedroom 1
12'-2" x 14'-10"
10'-0" Clg.

M. Bath
10'-0" Clg.

Entry
Beamed Clg.

WIC

Make-Up Area

Whirlpool

Walk-In Shower

Privacy Garden

Utility
5'-4" x 8'-4"
10'-0" Clg.

Garage
22'-0" x 31'-6"
10'-0" Clg.

©THE SATER DESIGN COLLECTION, INC.

rear elevation

© The Sater Design Collection, Inc.

Trevi

COUP DE MAITRE — *Massive stone turrets establish a stately street presence for this Italian villa, yet a sandals-only attitude weaves through the interior.*

Turrets frame the entry arcade of this magnificent manor. Inside, a lively mix of breezy, open spaces—rich with smart features—and high-glam rooms creates an at-home feeling that invites all kinds of gatherings. Crafted furnishings complement high-tech angles and panoramic views in new fusions of form and function. A through-fireplace anchors a living room that extends out into the veranda with three sets of French doors. Varied ceiling treatments define rooms that defy their boundaries with walls of glass and unrestrained spaces. Columns and soffits whisper the edges of a gallery colonnade that runs nearly the width of the plan. A splendid owners' retreat features a bumped-out marble oval tub and deck all with a garden view.

PLAN | *8065*

Bedroom: 4   Width: 95'0"

Bath: 3-1/2   Depth: 84'0"

Foundation: Slab or
  optional basement

Exterior Walls: 2x6

Main Level: 3,581 sq ft

Upper Level: 1,256 sq ft

Living Area: 4,837 sq ft

Price Code: **L2**

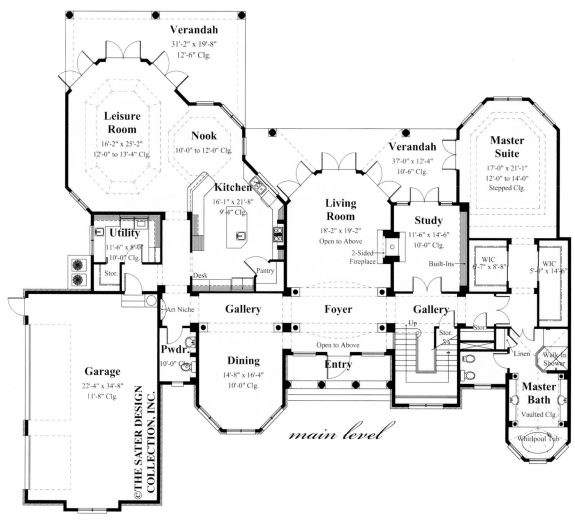

Verandah
31'-2" x 19'-8"
12'-6" Clg.

Leisure Room
16'-2" x 25'-2"
12'-0" to 13'-4" Clg.

Nook
10'-0" x 12'-0" Clg.

Kitchen
16'-1" x 21'-8"
9'-4" Clg.

Verandah
37'-0" x 12'-4"
10'-6" Clg.

Master Suite
17'-0" x 21'-1"
12'-0" to 14'-0"
Stepped Clg.

Utility
11'-6" x 8'-0"
10'-0" Clg.

Stor.

Living Room
18'-2" x 19'-2"
Open to Above

Study
11'-6" x 14'-6"
10'-0" Clg.

2-Sided Fireplace

Built-Ins

WIC
6'-7" x 8'-8"

WIC
5'-0" x 14'-6"

Desk

Pantry

Art Niche

Gallery

Foyer

Gallery

Up

Stor.

Stor.

Linen

Walk-In Shower

©THE SATER DESIGN COLLECTION, INC.

Garage
22'-4" x 34'-8"
11'-8" Clg.

Pwdr.
10'-0" Clg.

Dining
14'-8" x 16'-4"
10'-0" Clg.

Entry

Open to Above

Master Bath
Vaulted Clg.

Whirlpool Tub

main level

©THE SATER DESIGN COLLECTION, INC.

WIC

Balcony
12'-6" x 12'-4"

Balcony
16'-6" x 12'-4"

Bedroom 2
14'-11" x 16'-0"
9'-0" Clg.

Open to Below
Coffered Clg.

Bedroom 3
13'-0" x 14'-6"
9'-0" Clg.

Walk-In Shower

Walk-In Shower

Bath 2
9'-0" Clg.

WIC

Bath 3
9'-0" Clg.

WIC

Balcony
9'-0" Clg.

Art Niche

Dn.

Bedroom 4
14'-8" x 16'-4"
9'-0" Clg.

Open to Below

Balcony
18'-8" x 5'-8"

upper level

rear elevation

www.saterdesign.com

© The Sater Design Collection, Inc.

REGION/STYLE | *French*

Chateauesque, Normandy, and Renaissance—

here are hip revival styles that meld massive turrets,

stone gables and flared eaves with open galleries and grand staircases.

Finely sculpted entries and gentle arches

partner happily with flexible interiors.

This elegant portfolio of homes, inspired by a history-rich past,

is finely tuned to the future.

© The Sater Design Collection, Inc.

Royal Country Down

MODERN ATTITUDE — *Picturesque towers and renaissance forms transmit a 21st-century allure, with neo-aesthetics that don't think twice about days gone by.*

Massive masonry walls, checkered brick-and-stucco panels and semicircular stone pediments recall a classic Chateauesque motif that's the new darling of Euro architecture. Renaissance details—carved pilasters, rusticated columns and scrolled pediments—highlight the refined spirit of the home, which prevails beyond the grand entry. Formal spaces radiate from a splendid gallery of arches and columns—a deliberate strategy that permits the interior vistas to penetrate the skin of the elevation, past the rear veranda to the ocean or hills beyond. Built-in shelves frame an entertainment center in the leisure room, and anchor an open arrangement of casual space with the morning nook and gourmet kitchen. A spectacular yet comfortable winding staircase draws family members and guests up to the secondary sleeping quarters on the upper level. With a private deck, walk-in shower and spacious bedroom, a live-in relative will feel right at home.

PLAN | 8001

Bedroom: 4   Width: 85'0"

Bath: 3-1/2   Depth: 76'7"

Foundation: Slab or
   optional basement

Exterior Walls: 2x6

Main Level: 2,834 sq ft

Upper Level: 1,143 sq ft

Living Area: 3,977 sq ft

Price Code: **L1**

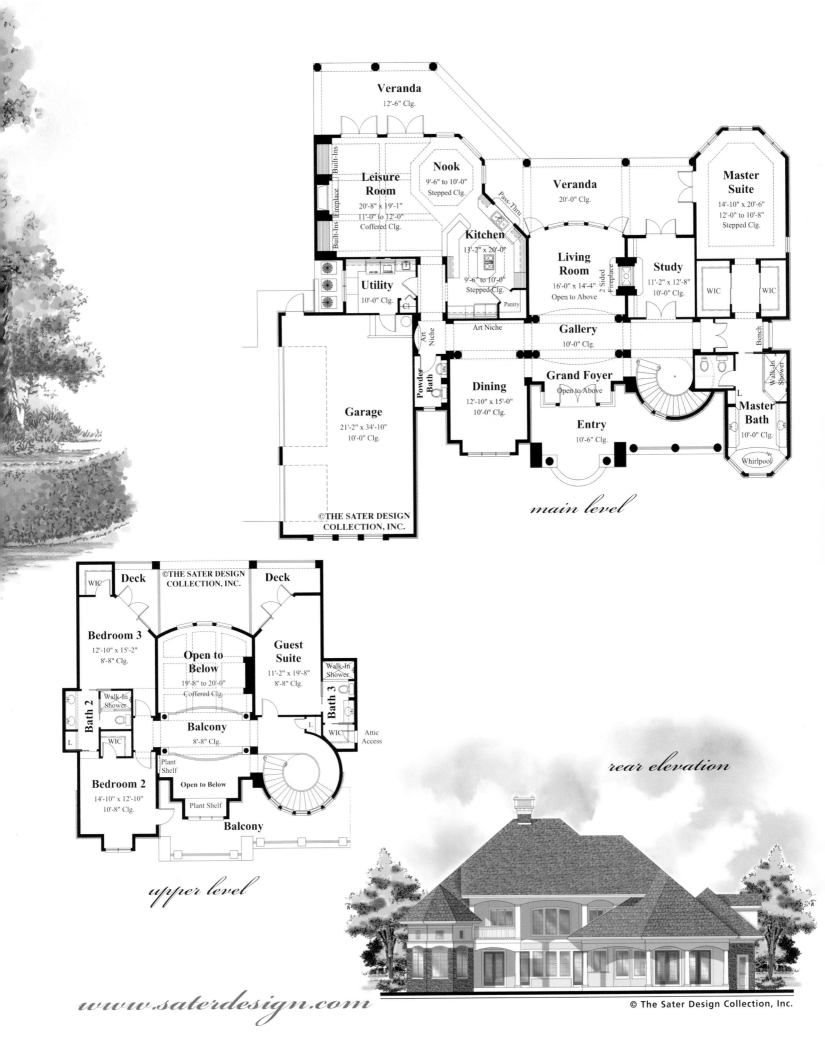

Veranda
12'-6" Clg.

Leisure Room
20'-8" x 19'-1"
11'-0" to 12'-0"
Coffered Clg.

Built-Ins

Built-Ins Fireplace

Nook
9'-6" to 10'-0"
Stepped Clg.

Veranda
20'-0" Clg.

Master Suite
14'-10" x 20'-6"
12'-0" to 10'-8"
Stepped Clg.

Pass-Thru

Kitchen
13'-2" x 20'-0"
9'-6" to 10'-0"
Stepped Clg.

Living Room
16'-0" x 14'-4"
Open to Above

2 Sided Fireplace

Study
11'-2" x 12'-8"
10'-0" Clg.

WIC   WIC

Utility
10'-0" Clg.

Cl

Pantry

Art Niche

Gallery
10'-0" Clg.

Bench

Art Niche

Powder Bath

Garage
21'-2" x 34'-10"
10'-0" Clg.

Dining
12'-10" x 15'-0"
10'-0" Clg.

Grand Foyer
Open to Above

Entry
10'-6" Clg.

Walk-In Shower

L

Master Bath
10'-0" Clg.

Whirlpool

©THE SATER DESIGN
COLLECTION, INC.

main level

Deck   ©THE SATER DESIGN COLLECTION, INC.   **Deck**

WIC

Bedroom 3
12'-10" x 15'-2"
8'-8" Clg.

Open to Below
19'-8" to 20'-0"
Coffered Clg.

Guest Suite
11'-2" x 19'-8"
8'-8" Clg.

Walk-In Shower

Walk-In Shower

Bath 2

WIC

Balcony
8'-8" Clg.

Bath 3

WIC

Attic Access

Bedroom 2
14'-10" x 12'-10"
10'-8" Clg.

Plant Shelf

Open to Below

Plant Shelf

Balcony

upper level

rear elevation

www.saterdesign.com

© The Sater Design Collection, Inc.

© The Sater Design Collection, Inc.

Channing

HEAVEN ON EARTH — *Familiar elements—shingles, brick and copper—join forces with this 21st-century Euro-flavored manor, creating sheer bliss from pure function.*

State-of-the-art amenities reside blissfully together with a spirit of artisanship in this rural French country home, announced by a wrapping portico, a shingled gable and copper-seam roofs. Inspired spaces flex from private to public, formal to comfortable. Pocket doors conceal a richly accoutered and entirely comfortable study, enhanced with a beamed ceiling and a bay window. Columns and arches articulate the formal dining room yet allow the space to mingle with interior vistas granted by the great room—a shoes-are-optional place that's right for planned events too. An angled master wing offers an art niche, a tray ceiling and French doors that lead to a terrace with an outdoor grille. Unique to this plan are a rear stair hall with a mud room, a windowed culinary pantry and an upper-level computer loft with a view of the great room.

PLAN	*8005*

Bedroom: 4   Width: 91'0"

Bath: 3-1/2   Depth: 52'8"

Foundation: Slab or
    optional basement

Exterior Walls: 2x6

Main Level: 2,219 sq ft

Upper Level: 1,088 sq ft

Living Area: 3,307 sq ft

Bonus Room: 446 sq ft

Price Code: **C4**

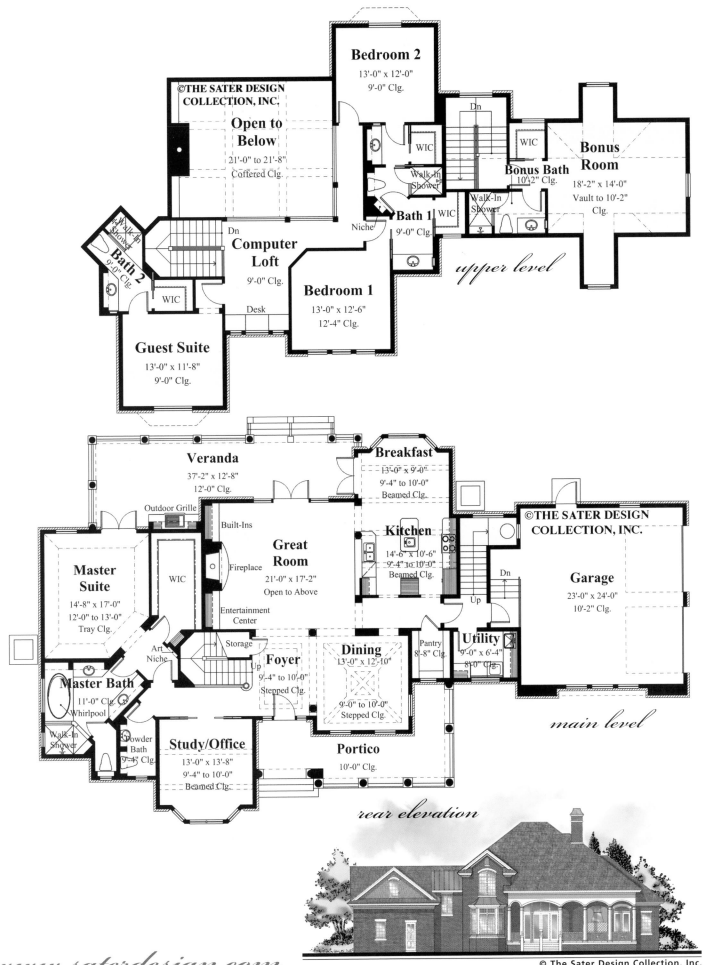

Bedroom 2
13'-0" x 12'-0"
9'-0" Clg.

©THE SATER DESIGN
COLLECTION, INC.

Dn

**Open to
Below**
21'-0" to 21'-8"
Coffered Clg.

WIC

WIC

**Bonus
Room**
18'-2" x 14'-0"
Vault to 10'-2"
Clg.

Walk-In
Shower

Bonus Bath
10'-2" Clg.

Bath 2
9'-0" Clg.

Walk-In
Shower

Dn

Bath 1
9'-0" Clg.

Walk-In
Shower

WIC

Niche

**Computer
Loft**
9'-0" Clg.

upper level

WIC

Desk

Bedroom 1
13'-0" x 12'-6"
12'-4" Clg.

Guest Suite
13'-0" x 11'-8"
9'-0" Clg.

Veranda
37'-2" x 12'-8"
12'-0" Clg.

Breakfast
13'-0" x 9'-0"
9'-4" to 10'-0"
Beamed Clg.

©THE SATER DESIGN
COLLECTION, INC.

Outdoor Grille

Built-Ins

Kitchen
14'-6" x 10'-6"
9'-4" to 10'-0"
Beamed Clg.

Fireplace

**Great
Room**
21'-0" x 17'-2"
Open to Above

**Master
Suite**
14'-8" x 17'-0"
12'-0" to 13'-0"
Tray Clg.

WIC

Garage
23'-0" x 24'-0"
10'-2" Clg.

Dn

Up

Entertainment
Center

Pantry
8'-8" Clg.

Utility
9'-0" x 6'-4"
8'-0" Clg.

Art
Niche

Storage

Up

Foyer
9'-4" to 10'-0"
Stepped Clg.

Dining
13'-0" x 12'-10"
9'-0" to 10'-0"
Stepped Clg.

Master Bath
11'-0" Clg.

Whirlpool

main level

Walk-In
Shower

Powder
Bath
9'-4" Clg.

Study/Office
13'-0" x 13'-8"
9'-4" to 10'-0"
Beamed Clg.

Portico
10'-0" Clg.

rear elevation

www.saterdesign.com

© The Sater Design Collection, Inc.

© The Sater Design Collection, Inc.

Baxter

JOIE D'VIVRE — *Neoclassic forms and rough stone walls surround joyful indoor/outdoor rooms with elegant grandeur designed for new neighborhoods.*

Rustic and venerable, this new Norman villa employs a mix of massive stone walls and ebullient details to create a spirit of elegant repose. A lovely arcade enhanced with fanlights and French doors leads to a grand interior that is oriented to rear vistas. Retreating walls, glass doors, and bow and bay windows permit plenty of natural light and spectacular views to fill the home. Classic materials and a historic style play well against extraordinary touches, such as a two-way fireplace, stepped ceilings and an angled entertainment center in the leisure room. A meld of authentic architectural details and cutting-edge technology prepares the gourmet kitchen for any culinary event—traditional dinners and quick snacks, as well as meals alfresco. Lavish embellishments adorn the owners' retreat: a windowed walk-in shower, dual wardrobe with storage, and a bumped-out whirlpool tub with views of a private garden.

PLAN | *8009*

Bedroom: 3   Width: 106'4"

Bath: 3-1/2   Depth: 102'4"

Foundation: Slab or
  optional basement

Exterior Walls: 2x6

Main Level: 3,640 sq ft

Living Area: 3,640 sq ft

Price Code: **L1**

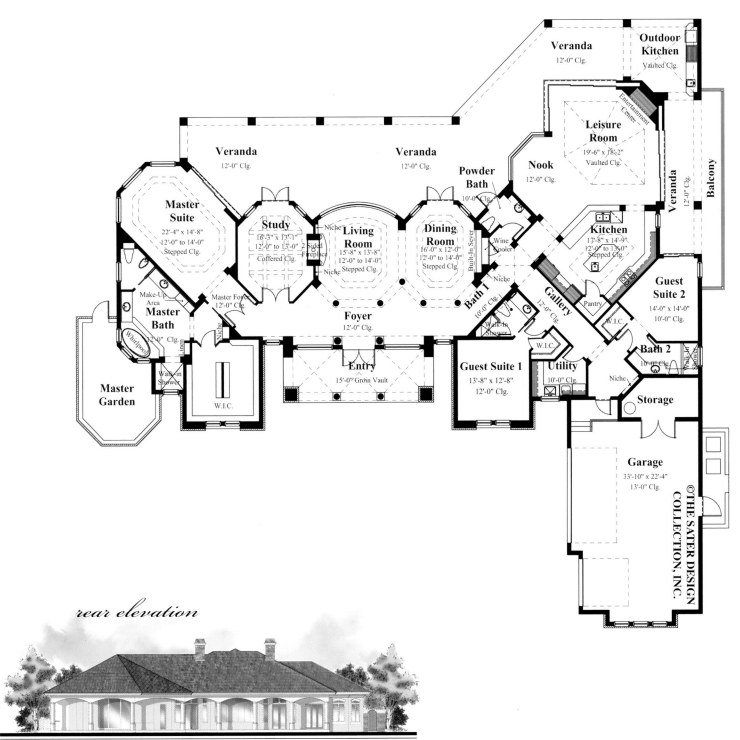

Veranda
12'-0" Clg.

Outdoor Kitchen
Vaulted Clg.

Veranda
12'-0" Clg.

Leisure Room
19'-6" x 18'-2"
Vaulted Clg.

Entertainment Center

Veranda
12'-0" Clg.

Balcony

Master Suite
22'-4" x 14'-8"
12'-0" to 14'-0"
Stepped Clg.

Veranda
12'-0" Clg.

Veranda
12'-0" Clg.

Powder Bath
10'-0" Clg.

Nook
12'-0" Clg.

Study
16'-3" x 13'-1"
12'-0" to 13'-0"
Coffered Clg.

Niche

Living Room
15'-8" x 13'-8"
12'-0" to 14'-0"
Stepped Clg.

2 Sided Fireplace

Niche

Dining Room
16'-0" x 12'-0"
12'-0" to 14'-0"
Stepped Clg.

Wine Cooler

Built-In Server

Niche

Kitchen
17'-8" x 14'-9"
12'-0" to 18'-0"
Stepped Clg.

Guest Suite 2
14'-0" x 14'-0"
10'-0" Clg.

Make-Up Area

Master Bath
13'-0" Clg.

Whirlpool

Master Foyer
12'-0" Clg.

Master Foyer
12'-0" Clg.

Niche

Foyer
12'-0" Clg.

Bath 1
10'-0" Clg.

Gallery
12'-0" Clg.

Pantry

W.I.C.

Bath 2
10'-0" Clg.

Linen

Walk-In Shower

Master Garden

Walk-In Shower

W.I.C.

Entry
15'-0" Groin Vault

Guest Suite 1
13'-8" x 12'-8"
12'-0" Clg.

W.I.C.

Utility
10'-0" Clg.

Niche

Storage

© THE SATER DESIGN COLLECTION, INC.

Garage
33'-10" x 22'-4"
13'-0" Clg.

rear elevation

© The Sater Design Collection, Inc.

with walkout basement

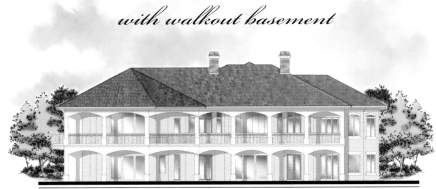

© The Sater Design Collection, Inc.

www.saterdesign.com

French | NORMANDY

© The Sater Design Collection, Inc.

La Riviere

FRENCH TWIST — *A rusticated entry surround and rugged stone evoke the eclectic styles of 19th-century France—yet this home is designed for the future.*

Arched windows and elegant dormers set off a rich blend of clapboard, stucco and stone with this New World villa, and establish a sense of the French tradition. Varied rooflines accentuate the timeless appeal of the blended elevation yet speak to a style that's meant for today's neighborhoods. An open arrangement of the public zone secures panoramic views within each of the formal spaces. The living room boasts a sense of nature granted through a two-story bow window, framed by bay windows in the morning nook and the sitting area of the master suite. A lavish garden bath in the owners' retreat echoes the outdoors-in theme found throughout the home. On the upper level, a spacious computer loft links the family's sleeping quarters with a guest suite and a step-down bonus room.

PLAN | *8011*

Bedroom: 4   Width: 71'6"
Bath: 4-1/2   Depth: 83'0"
Foundation: Slab or
   optional basement
Exterior Walls: 2x6

Main Level: 2,850 sq ft
Upper Level: 1,155 sq ft

Living Area: 4,005 sq ft
Bonus Room: 371 sq ft

Price Code: **L2**

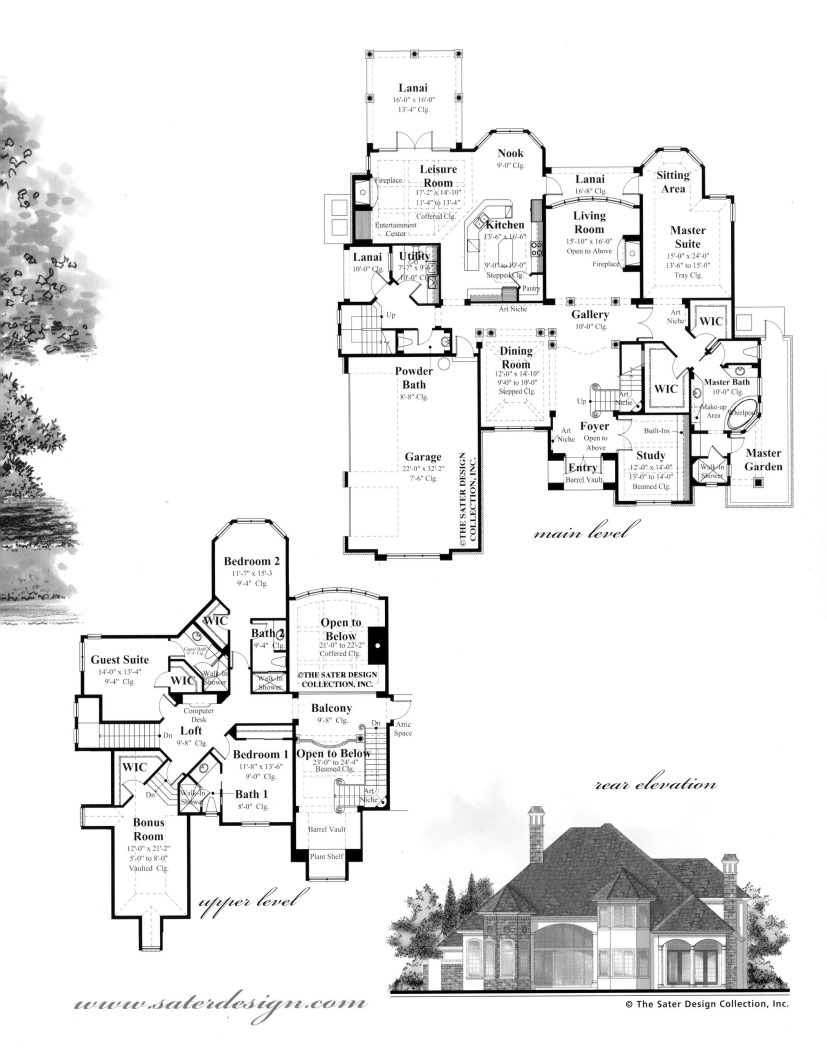

Burke House

BRAVE HEART — *Bold and simply beautiful, this French Country manor promises 21st-century repose for commuters, couples and city dwellers.*

Decorative diamond-pane windows set off the entry turret of this Euro-style home, announced by a pedimented entry that suggests a renaissance influence. A progressive interior explores the integration of romantic Old World elements and cutting-edge architecture. In the center of the plan, a dramatic stepped ceiling plays counterpoint to an energy-saving through-fireplace shared by the great room and study. Walls of glass define the rear perimeter of the plan, permitting views and light throughout the home. A food-prep island, walk-in pantry and wrapping counters highlight a well-planned kitchen, which adjoins a wet bar and servery leading to the formal dining room. Upstairs, two grand lofts harbor space for homework, computers and books. Timber beams extend beyond the balcony loft to the vaulted leisure room on the main level. Family suites complement splendid guest quarters, which boast a private balcony.

PLAN	*8015*

Bedroom: 4   Width: 70'0"

Bath: 4-1/2   Depth: 100'0"

Foundation: Slab or
   optional basement

Exterior Walls: 2x6

Main Level: 3,023 sq ft

Upper Level: 1,623 sq ft

Living Area: 4,646 sq ft

Bonus Room: 294 sq ft

Price Code: **L2**

Open to Below
Vaulted Clg.

Balcony

Guest Suite
12'-0" x 13'-2"
9'-0" to 10'-0"
Tray Clg.

Open to Below
20'-8" to 22'-0"
Coffered Clg.

Loft
9'-0" to 10'-8"
Beamed Clg.

Opt. Bedroom
15'-11" x 14'-2"
10'-8" Clg.

WIC

WIC

Walk-In
Shower

Art
Niche

Loft

Dn.

Art
Niche

Walk-In
Shower

Bath
9'-0" Clg.

Bath 3
9'-0" Clg.

loft / bedroom option

Dome Clg.

Dn.

Bedroom 1
12'-8" x 17'-3"
9'-0" to 10'-8"
Vaulted Clg.

WIC

Bath
9'-0" Clg.

Bedroom 2
11'-6" x 15'-0"
10'-8" Clg.

Walk-In
Shower

WIC

upper level

WIC

Bonus Room
12'-0" x 15'-10"
Vault to 8'-0" Clg.

Veranda
18'-0" x 15'-6"
Vaulted Clg.

Entertainment
Center

Leisure Room
17'-0" x 20'-6"
Open to Above

Fireplace

Built-Ins

Master Suite
13'-0" x 18'-7"
12'-0" to 13'-0"
Tray Clg.

Veranda
13'-0" x 9'-0"
10'-0" Clg.

Nook
9'-0" x 7'-0"
Open to Above

Study
12'-0" x 13'-2"
9'-0" to 10'-0"
Stepped Clg.

Living Room
15'-6" x 16'-4"
Open to Above
2-Sided Fireplace

Up

Kitchen
16'-10" x 14'-8"
9'-4" to 10'-0"
Stepped Clg.

WIC

Pantry

WIC

Art
Niche

Storage

Gallery
10'-0" Clg.

**Wet
Bar**
10'-0" Clg.

Utility
7'-6" x 10'-0"
10'-0" Clg.

Master Bath
11'-0" to 12'-0"
Stepped Clg.

Up

Open to
Above

Dining
12'-8" x 17'-3"
9'-0" to 10'-0"
Stepped Clg.

Storage

Pwdr.
10'-0" Clg.

Privacy
Garden

Whirlpool

Walk-In
Shower

Foyer
10'-0" Clg.

Garage
22'-0" x 31'-0"
10'-0" Clg.

Entry
10'-0" Clg.

main level

rear elevation

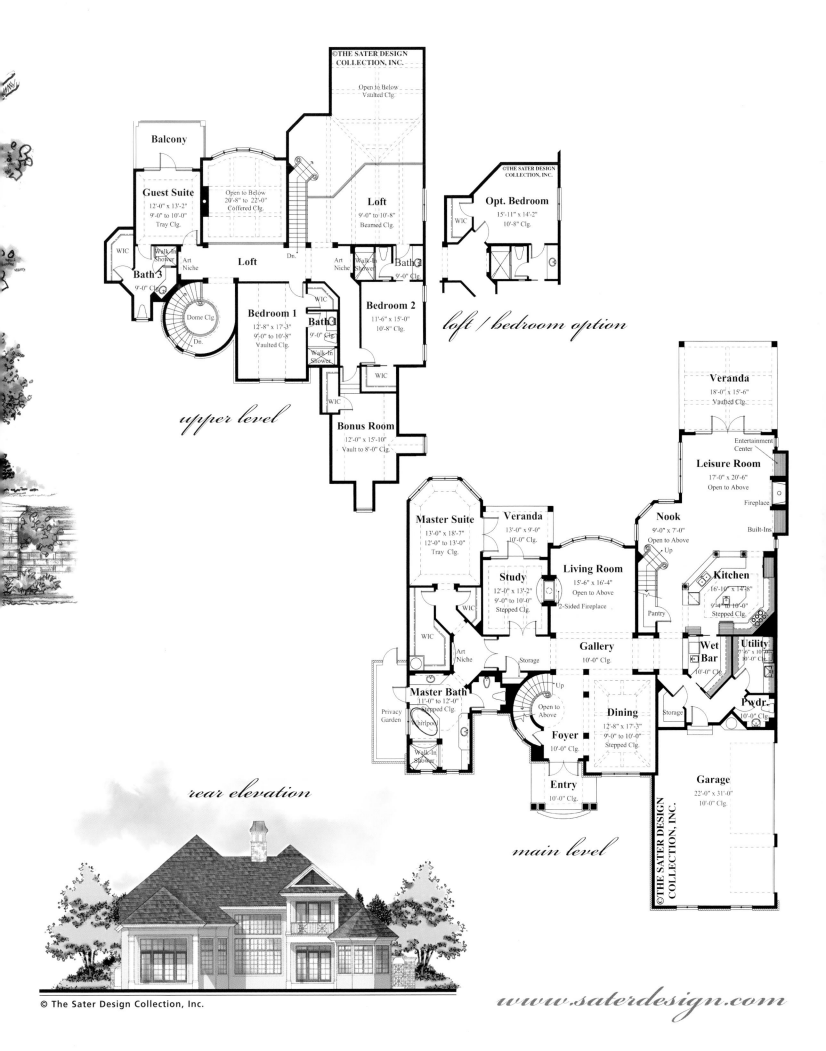

www.saterdesign.com

© The Sater Design Collection, Inc.

Les Tourelles

TOWN AND COUNTRY — *Fine lines and elegant masonry embellish a richly detailed French Revival facade, rooted in the past yet ready for the future.*

A steeply pitched roof caps artful porticos reminiscent of the early French houses of the southeastern coastal regions. Double columns, and decorative railings borrow freely from the past, while a thoughtfully placed turret reinvents traffic flow within. Formal rooms flank the foyer and open to the gallery in a traditional arrangement of the public zone. A high-glam tower staircase placed axially to the entry brings in natural light. At the center of the plan, great views dominate the two-story leisure room, which leads out to the lanai. In the owners' retreat, a magnificent bay window and a French door bring in a sense of nature, while a private foyer and a morning kitchen maintain privacy. On the upper level, a balcony hall sports built-in shelves and a computer desk—all brightened by natural light from the stair tower. Bedroom 2 brags a walk-in shower and access to a private deck.

PLAN | *8017*

Bedroom: 4   Width: 83'0"
Bath: 3-1/2   Depth: 71'8"
Foundation: Slab or
  optional basement
Exterior Walls: 2x6

Main Level: 2,481 sq ft
Upper Level: 1,132 sq ft

Living Area: 3,613 sq ft
Bonus Room: 332 sq ft

Price Code: **L1**

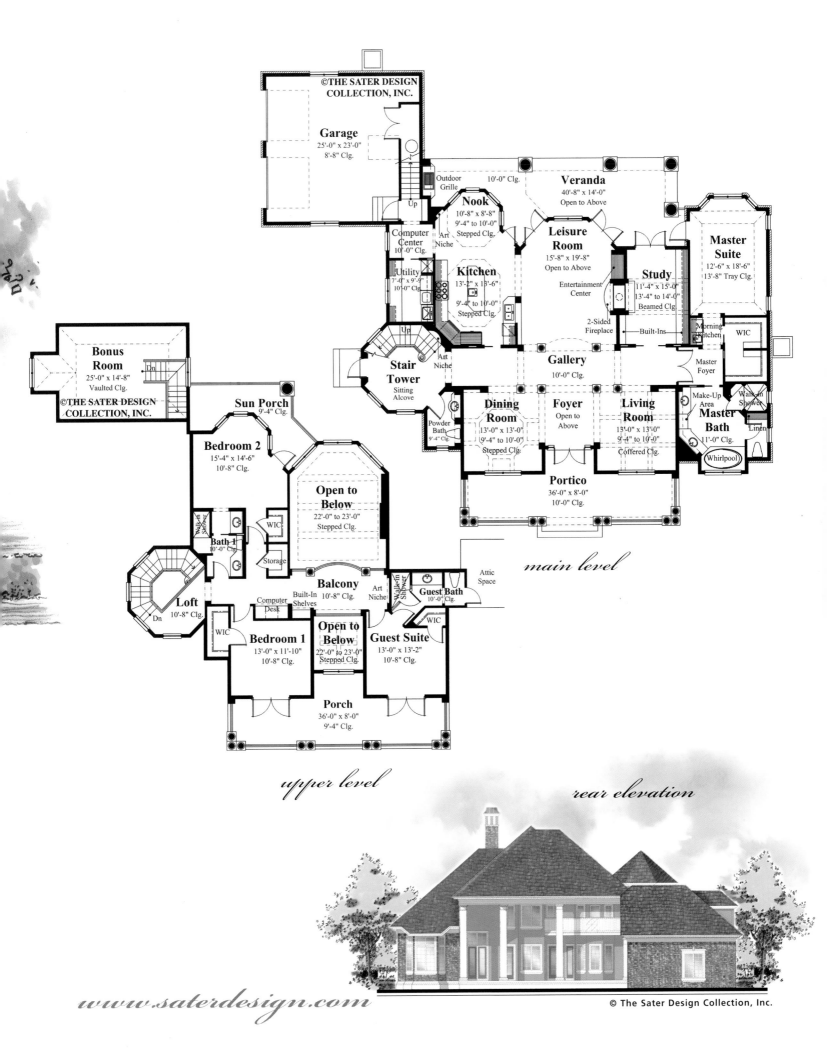

Garage
25'-0" x 23'-0"
8'-8" Clg.

©THE SATER DESIGN
COLLECTION, INC.

Outdoor
Grille

10'-0" Clg.

Veranda
40'-8" x 14'-0"
Open to Above

Nook
10'-8" x 8'-8"
9'-4" to 10'-0"
Stepped Clg.

**Leisure
Room**
15'-8" x 19'-8"
Open to Above

**Master
Suite**
12'-6" x 18'-6"
13'-8" Tray Clg.

Computer
Center
10'-0" Clg.

Art
Niche

Utility
7'-0" x 9'-9"
10'-0" Clg.

Kitchen
13'-2" x 13'-6"
9'-4" to 10'-0"
Stepped Clg.

Study
11'-4" x 15'-0"
13'-4" to 14'-0"
Beamed Clg.

Entertainment
Center

Morning
Kitchen

WIC

Up

**Stair
Tower**
Sitting
Alcove

Art
Niche

2-Sided
Fireplace

Built-Ins

Gallery
10'-0" Clg.

Master
Foyer

Make-Up
Area

Walk-In
Shower

Powder
Bath
9'-4" Clg.

**Dining
Room**
13'-0" x 13'-0"
9'-4" to 10'-0"
Stepped Clg.

Foyer
Open to
Above

**Living
Room**
13'-0" x 13'-0"
9'-4" to 10'-0"
Coffered Clg.

**Master
Bath**
11'-0" Clg.

Linen

Whirlpool

Portico
36'-0" x 8'-0"
10'-0" Clg.

main level

**Bonus
Room**
25'-0" x 14'-8"
Vaulted Clg.

Dn

©THE SATER DESIGN
COLLECTION, INC.

Sun Porch
9'-4" Clg.

Bedroom 2
15'-4" x 14'-6"
10'-8" Clg.

**Open to
Below**
22'-0" to 23'-0"
Stepped Clg.

WIC

Bath 1
10'-0" Clg.

Storage

Loft
10'-8" Clg.

Dn

WIC

Bedroom 1
13'-0" x 11'-10"
10'-8" Clg.

Computer
Desk

Built-In
Shelves

Balcony
10'-8" Clg.

Art
Niche

Walk-In Shower

**Guest
Bath**
10'-0"

Attic
Space

WIC

**Open to
Below**
22'-0" to 23'-0"
Stepped Clg.

Guest Suite
13'-0" x 13'-2"
10'-8" Clg.

Porch
36'-0" x 8'-0"
9'-4" Clg.

upper level

rear elevation

© The Sater Design Collection, Inc.

Bellamy

ALMOST HEAVEN — *Leaf-hued stucco and cloud-toned masonry parlay a palette of earth tones against a splendid presentation of order, symmetry and balance.*

Well-crafted millwork, pediments and ornamented dormers reinforce a distinctive Chateauesque theme with this vernacular design. An elaborated chimney stands sentinel above a high multi-pitched roof, and complements a massive side turret. Transoms and fanlights extend the motif outside, and lend texture and natural light to the interior. A sense of French tradition is reiterated in the public realm with an enfilade arrangement of rooms, with the living and dining rooms opposite the leisure room and study. The home steps boldly into the future, though, with such up-to-the-minute amenities as a two-way fireplace, a six-burner cooktop and food-prep counter, a computer loft and walk-in everything. Positioned to the side of the plan, a winding staircase employs the turret to bring natural light to the main and upper galleries.

PLAN	*8018*

Bedroom: 4	Width: 83'0"
Bath: 3-1/2	Depth: 71'8"
Foundation: Slab or optional basement	
Exterior Walls: 2x6	
Main Level: 2,483 sq ft	
Upper Level: 1,127 sq ft	
Living Area: 3,610 sq ft	
Bonus Room: 332 sq ft	
Price Code: **L1**	

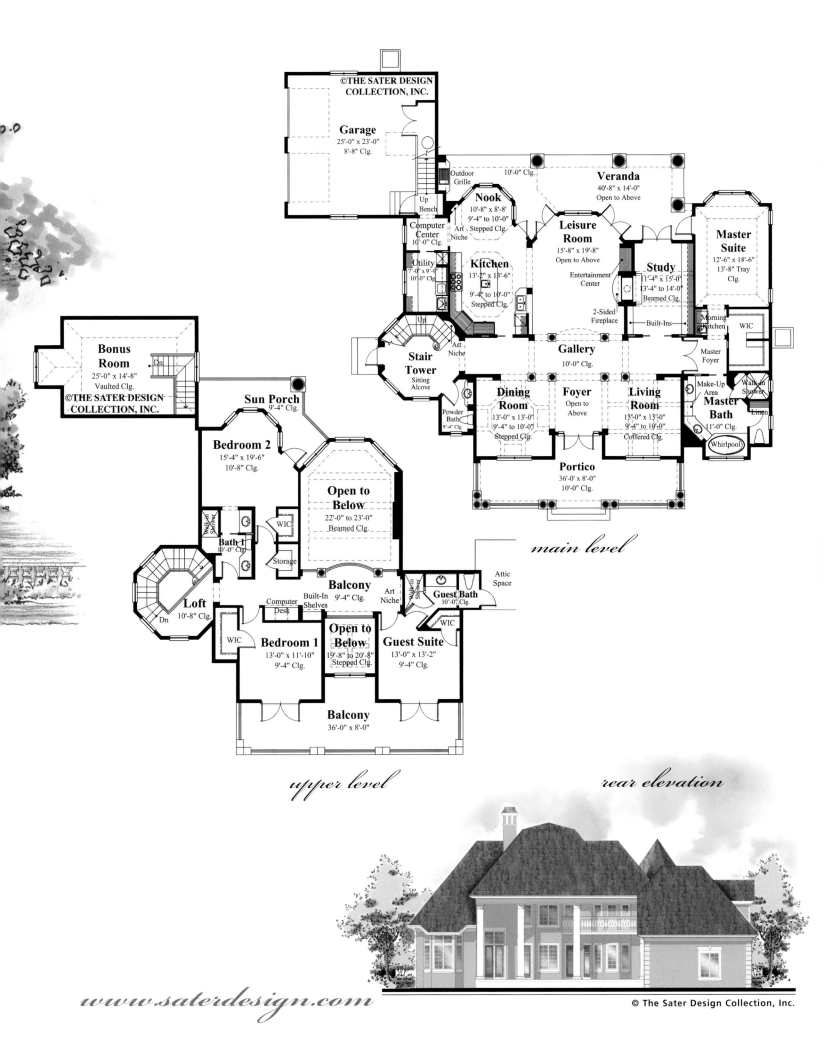

©THE Sater Design
COLLECTION, INC.

Garage
25'-0" x 23'-0"
8'-8" Clg.

Up
Bench

Computer
Center
10'-0" Clg.

Outdoor
Grille

Art Niche

Nook
10'-8" x 8'-8'
9'-4" to 10'-0"
Stepped Clg.

10'-0" Clg.

Veranda
40'-8" x 14'-0"
Open to Above

**Leisure
Room**
15'-8" x 19'-8"
Open to Above

**Master
Suite**
12'-6" x 18'-6"
13'-8" Tray
Clg.

Utility
7'-0" x 9'-9"
10'-0" Clg.

Kitchen
13'-2" x 13'-6"
9'-4" to 10'-0"
Stepped Clg.

Entertainment
Center

Study
11'-4" x 15'-0"
13'-4" to 14'-0"
Beamed Clg.

Morning
Kitchen

WIC

2-Sided
Fireplace

Built-Ins

**Stair
Tower**
Sitting
Alcove

Up

Art
Niche

Gallery
10'-0" Clg.

Master
Foyer

Master
Foyer

Make-Up
Area

Walk-In
Shower

Powder
Bath
9'-4" Clg.

**Dining
Room**
13'-0" x 13'-0"
9'-4" to 10'-0"
Stepped Clg.

Foyer
Open to
Above

**Living
Room**
13'-0" x 13'-0"
9'-4" to 10'-0"
Coffered Clg.

**Master
Bath**
11'-0" Clg.

Linen

Whirlpool

Portico
36'-0" x 8'-0"
10'-0" Clg.

main level

**Bonus
Room**
25'-0" x 14'-8"
Vaulted Clg.

Dn

©THE Sater Design
COLLECTION, INC.

Sun Porch
9'-4" Clg.

Bedroom 2
15'-4" x 19'-6"
10'-8" Clg.

**Open to
Below**
22'-0" to 23'-0"
Beamed Clg.

Walk-In
Shower

WIC

Bath 1
10'-0" Clg.

Storage

Loft
10'-8" Clg.

Dn

Computer
Desk

Built-In
Shelves

Balcony
9'-4" Clg.

Art
Niche

Walk-In
Shower

Guest Bath
10'-0" Clg.

Attic
Space

WIC

WIC

Bedroom 1
13'-0" x 11'-10"
9'-4" Clg.

**Open to
Below**
19'-8" to 20'-8"
Stepped Clg.

Guest Suite
13'-0" x 13'-2"
9'-4" Clg.

Balcony
36'-0" x 8'-0"

upper level

rear elevation

© The Sater Design Collection, Inc.

New Brunswick

DOMESTIC BLISS — *Sweet symmetry surrounds a double portico on a distinctly American facade that's rooted in a rich European past.*

Snow-white stucco creates a perfect complement to this traditional red brick facade. The front porch colonnade is flanked by two copper topped bay windows. Much more than a beautiful enhancement of the streetscape, this stately design embraces 21st-century lifestyles with a deep level of comfort. A grand foyer opens to the perfect balance of well-defined formal rooms and inviting casual spaces. The prevalent use of natural light is a primary objective in the design—French doors and bay windows surround the main-level plan, while well-placed windows and access to outdoor places brighten the upper level. Guest accommodations include a spacious suite with a tray ceiling and access to a private deck.

PLAN | *8021*

Bedroom: 4   Width: 80'0"

Bath: 4-1/2   Depth: 63'8"

Foundation: Slab or
   optional basement

Exterior Walls: 2x6

Main Level: 2,232 sq ft

Upper Level: 1,269 sq ft

Living Area: 3,501 sq ft

Price Code: **L1**

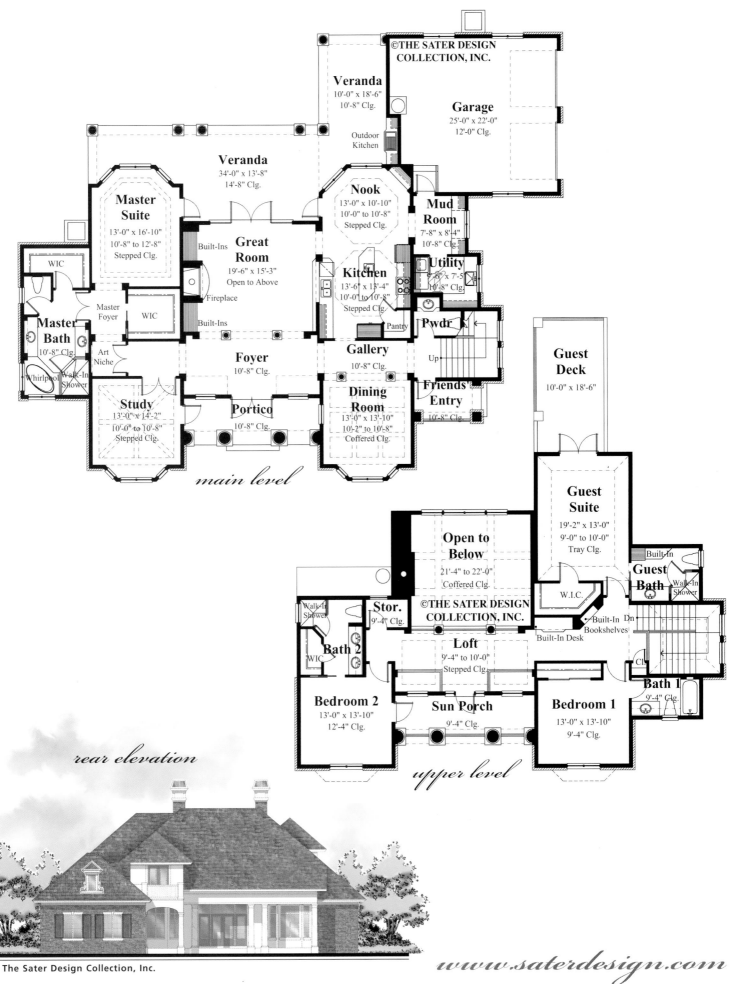

Veranda
10'-0" x 18'-6"
10'-8" Clg.

©THE SATER DESIGN
COLLECTION, INC.

Garage
25'-0" x 22'-0"
12'-0" Clg.

Outdoor
Kitchen

Veranda
34'-0" x 13'-8"
14'-8" Clg.

Nook
13'-0" x 10'-10"
10'-0" to 10'-8"
Stepped Clg.

Mud Room
7'-8" x 8'-4"
10'-8" Clg.

Master Suite
13'-0" x 16'-10"
10'-8" to 12'-8"
Stepped Clg.

WIC

Great Room
19'-6" x 15'-3"
Open to Above

Built-Ins

Fireplace

Built-Ins

Kitchen
13'-6" x 13'-4"
10'-0" to 10'-8"
Stepped Clg.

Utility
9'-6" x 7'-5"
10'-8" Clg.

Master Foyer

WIC

Master Bath
10'-8" Clg.

Whirlpool

Walk-In Shower

Art Niche

Pantry

Pwdr

Up

Foyer
10'-8" Clg.

Gallery
10'-8" Clg.

Friends' Entry
10'-8" Clg.

Guest Deck
10'-0" x 18'-6"

Study
13'-0" x 14'-2"
10'-0" to 10'-8"
Stepped Clg.

Portico
10'-8" Clg.

Dining Room
13'-0" x 13'-10"
10'-2" to 10'-8"
Coffered Clg.

main level

Guest Suite
19'-2" x 13'-0"
9'-0" to 10'-0"
Tray Clg.

Built In

Open to Below
21'-4" to 22'-0"
Coffered Clg.

W.I.C.

Guest Bath

Walk-In Shower

Walk-In Shower

Stor.
9'-4" Clg.

©THE SATER DESIGN
COLLECTION, INC.

Built-In Desk

Built-In Bookshelves

Dn

Bath 2

WIC

Loft
9'-4" to 10'-0"
Stepped Clg.

Bath 1
9'-4" Clg.

Bedroom 2
13'-0" x 13'-10"
12'-4" Clg.

Sun Porch
9'-4" Clg.

Bedroom 1
13'-0" x 13'-10"
9'-4" Clg.

upper level

rear elevation

© The Sater Design Collection, Inc.

www.saterdesign.com

© The Sater Design Collection, Inc.

Gabriel

NEW NORMAN — *Rich with Romanesque beauty and 19th-century neo-Norman style, this classic French Country home is ready to sink roots in a new region.*

From the outside, this magnificent manor appears both familiar and fresh, as if its stately countenance were situated among chateaux on the Loire—both fitting and revising the look of the region. Masonry arches and massive stone gables frame an airy arcade, which harbors a symmetry of doors. The center door leads to a gallery foyer and great room, anchored by a massive fireplace and a thoroughly 21st-century entertainment center. French doors open to a terrace, fountain and courtyard; a spa and pool may be added. To the left of the plan, a loggia harbors an outdoor grille and eating area, which can be accessed from the morning nook and kitchen. Upstairs, a computer deck overlooks the great room and links the secondary suites. A rear deck leads to a splendid bonus room with a glass stair bay.

PLAN | 8024

Bedroom: 3   Width: 60'6"

Bath: 2-1/2   Depth: 94'0"

Foundation: Slab or
   optional basement

Exterior Walls: 2x6

Main Level: 2,084 sq ft

Upper Level: 652 sq ft

Living Area: 2,736 sq ft

Bonus Room: 365 sq ft

Price Code: **C3**

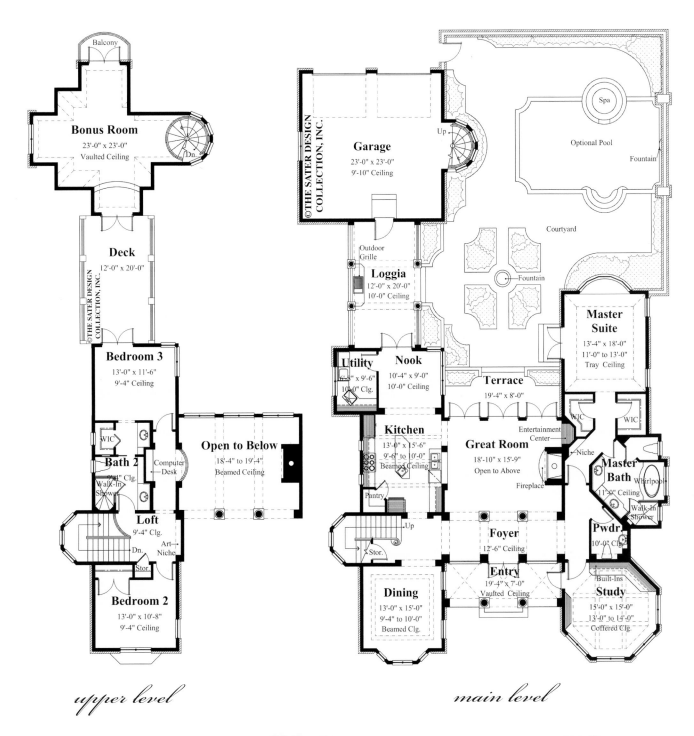

Bonus Room
23'-0" x 23'-0"
Vaulted Ceiling

Balcony

Dn.

Deck
12'-0" x 20'-0"

©THE SATER DESIGN COLLECTION, INC.

Bedroom 3
13'-0" x 11'-6"
9'-4" Ceiling

WIC

Open to Below
18'-4" to 19'-4"
Beamed Ceiling

Bath 2
9'-4" Clg.
Walk-In Shower

Computer Desk

Loft
9'-4" Clg.

Art Niche

Dn.

Stor.

Bedroom 2
13'-0" x 10'-8"
9'-4" Ceiling

upper level

©THE SATER DESIGN COLLECTION, INC.

Garage
23'-0" x 23'-0"
9'-10" Ceiling

Up

Spa

Optional Pool

Fountain

Outdoor Grille

Loggia
12'-0" x 20'-0"
10'-0" Ceiling

Fountain

Courtyard

Utility
6'-8" x 9'-6"
10'-0" Clg.

Nook
10'-4" x 9'-0"
10'-0" Ceiling

Terrace
19'-4" x 8'-0"

Master Suite
13'-4" x 18'-0"
11'-0" to 13'-0"
Tray Ceiling

WIC

WIC

Kitchen
13'-0" x 15'-6"
9'-6" to 10'-0"
Beamed Ceiling

Entertainment Center

Great Room
18'-10" x 15'-9"
Open to Above

Niche

Master Bath
Whirlpool
11'-0" Ceiling

Pantry

Fireplace

Walk-In Shower

Up

Foyer
12'-6" Ceiling

Pwdr.
10'-0" Clg.

Stor.

Dining
13'-0" x 15'-0"
9'-4" to 10'-0"
Beamed Clg.

Entry
19'-4" x 7'-0"
Vaulted Ceiling

Built-Ins

Study
15'-0" x 15'-0"
13'-0" to 14'-0"
Coffered Clg.

main level

rear elevation

www.saterdesign.com

© The Sater Design Collection, Inc.

© The Sater Design Collection, Inc.

St. Germain

HIP CHATEAU — *Inspired by rural Euro homes of ages past, this picturesque French Eclectic manor takes its cues from the techno-savvy days ahead.*

As steeped in artistry outside as it is state-of-the-art within, this dreamy villa blends bark-hued shingles with yellow brick and cream-white stucco—mixing forms such as flared eaves, slump arches and semi-hexagonal turret. Sculpted outdoor places lend definition and dignity to the elevation, reiterating a highly crafted interior. At the heart of the home, flexible public spaces take on an elegant formality for planned events, yet offer a bare-feet-only comfort zone for family members and friends. Nearby, the library/study employs a stepped ceiling and built-in shelves to provide texture and definition—relieved by double doors that open to the veranda. Upstairs, a wraparound loft overlooks the living space and links generous secondary quarters to the owners' retreat. A convenient elevator complements the high-glam staircase, which winds upward from the grand foyer.

PLAN | 8026

Bedroom: 5   Width: 58'0"

Bath: 5-1/2   Depth: 65'0"

Foundation: Slab or
   optional basement

Exterior Walls: 2x6

Main Level: 1,996 sq ft

Upper Level: 2,171 sq ft

Living Area: 4,167 sq ft

Price Code: **L2**

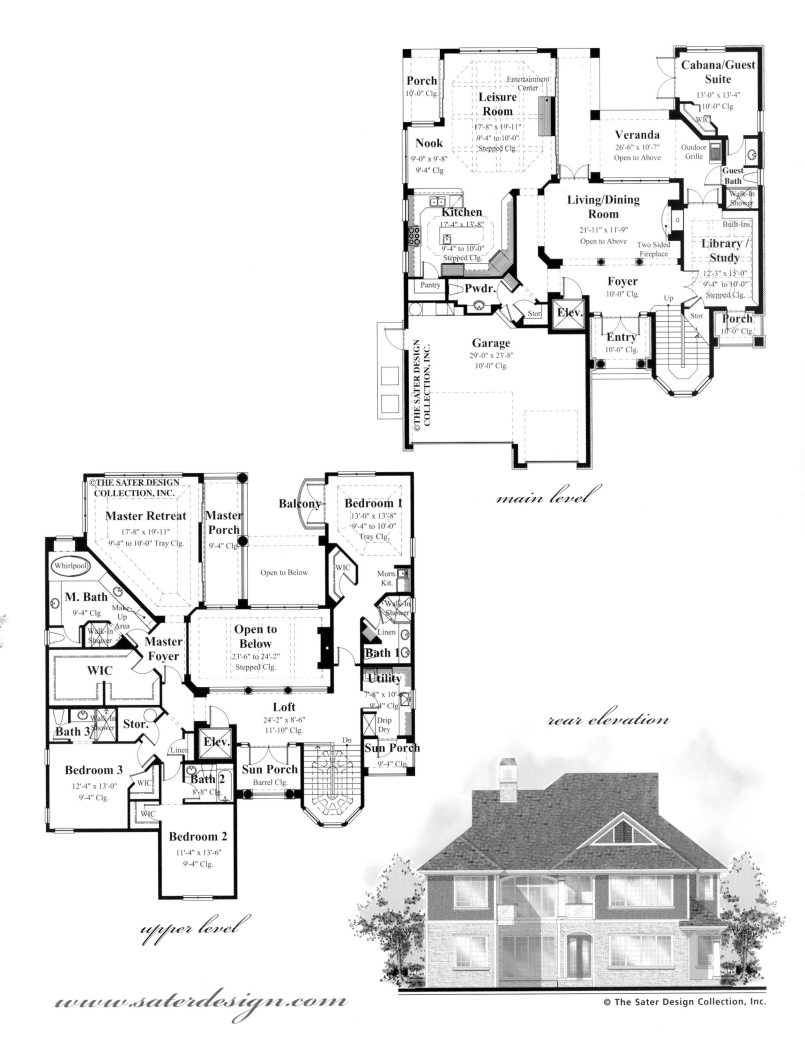

Porch
10'-0" Clg.

Leisure Room
17'-8" x 19'-11"
9'-4" to 10'-0"
Stepped Clg.

Entertainment Center

Cabana/Guest Suite
13'-0" x 13'-4"
10'-0" Clg.

WIC

Nook
9'-0" x 9'-8"
9'-4" Clg.

Veranda
26'-6" x 10'-7"
Open to Above

Outdoor Grille

Guest Bath

Walk-In Shower

Kitchen
17'-4" x 13'-8"
9'-4" to 10'-0"
Stepped Clg.

Living/Dining Room
21'-11" x 11'-9"
Open to Above

Built-Ins

Library / Study
12'-3" x 15'-0"
9'-4" to 10'-0"
Stepped Clg.

Two Sided Fireplace

Pantry

Pwdr.

Foyer
10'-0" Clg.

Stor.

Elev.

Up

Stor.

Porch
10'-0" Clg.

Garage
29'-0" x 23'-8"
10'-0" Clg.

Entry
10'-0" Clg.

main level

©THE SATER DESIGN COLLECTION, INC.

Master Retreat
17'-8" x 19'-11"
9'-4" to 10'-0" Tray Clg.

Master Porch
9'-4" Clg.

Balcony

Bedroom 1
13'-0" x 13'-8"
9'-4" to 10'-0"
Tray Clg.

Whirlpool

M. Bath
9'-4" Clg.

Make-Up Area

Open to Below

WIC

Morn. Kit.

Walk-In Shower

Walk-In Shower

Master Foyer

Open to Below
23'-6" to 24'-2"
Stepped Clg.

Linen

Bath 1

WIC

Utility
7'-8" x 10'-4"
9'-4" Clg.

Bath 3

Stor.

Linen

Elev.

Loft
24'-2" x 8'-6"
11'-10" Clg.

Drip Dry

Bedroom 3
12'-4" x 13'-0"
9'-4" Clg.

WIC

Bath 2
8'-8" Clg.

Sun Porch

Dn

Sun Porch
9'-4" Clg.

Sun Porch
Barrel Clg.

WIC

Bedroom 2
11'-4" x 13'-6"
9'-4" Clg.

upper level

rear elevation

www.saterdesign.com

© The Sater Design Collection, Inc.

Kinsley

SIMPLY PARADISE — *Wrought-iron railings and a Norman-style architecture step into the future with a stately elevation that promises all the comforts of home.*

A dual-pitched hip roof and gently arched dormers create the kind of new-old curb appeal that can transform a streetscape and revive an entire neighborhood. Natural textures of brick and stone play counterpoint to revival elements, suggesting a neoclassic influence. The home is entered through a deep foyer, which links axially to the central gallery hall and leads forward to a refined interior. Formal rooms grant a strong visual connection to the outdoors, with the exception of the study, which is secluded by pocket doors and designed for conversation. A massive, rugged fireplace and beamed ceiling offers an authentic presence and texture in the great room. Drawing on coastal vernaculars, the rear of the home opens to the veranda—an opportunity to allow the interior to mingle with light and breezes outside.

PLAN | *8030*

Bedroom: 3   Width: 62'10"

Bath: 2-1/2   Depth: 73'6"

Foundation: Slab or
    optional basement

Exterior Walls: 2x6

Main Level: 2,191 sq ft

Living Area: 2,191 sq ft

Price Code: **C2**

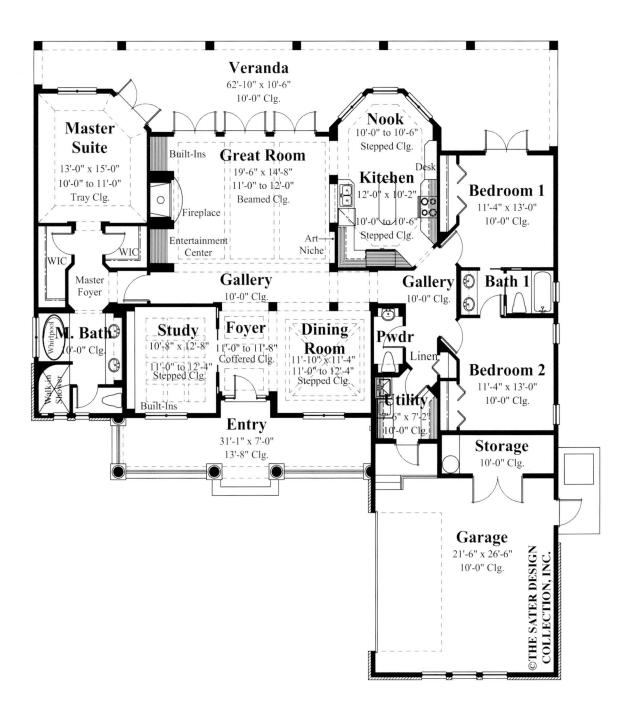

Veranda
62'-10" x 10'-6"
10'-0" Clg.

Master Suite
13'-0" x 15'-0"
10'-0" to 11'-0"
Tray Clg.

Built-Ins

Great Room
19'-6" x 14'-8"
11'-0" to 12'-0"
Beamed Clg.

Nook
10'-0" to 10'-6"
Stepped Clg.

Kitchen
12'-0" x 10'-2"
10'-0" to 10'-6"
Stepped Clg.

Desk

Bedroom 1
11'-4" x 13'-0"
10'-0" Clg.

Fireplace

Entertainment Center

Art Niche

WIC

WIC

Master Foyer

Gallery
10'-0" Clg.

Gallery
10'-0" Clg.

Bath 1

M. Bath
10'-0" Clg.

Whirlpool

Study
10'-8" x 12'-8"
11'-0" to 12'-4"
Stepped Clg.

Foyer
11'-0" to 11'-8"
Coffered Clg.

Dining Room
11'-10" x 11'-4"
11'-0" to 12'-4"
Stepped Clg.

Pwdr

Linen

Bedroom 2
11'-4" x 13'-0"
10'-0" Clg.

Walk-in Shower

Built-Ins

Utility
6" x 7'-2"
10'-0" Clg.

Entry
31'-1" x 7'-0"
13'-8" Clg.

Storage
10'-0" Clg.

Garage
21'-6" x 26'-6"
10'-0" Clg.

rear elevation

www.saterdesign.com

© The Sater Design Collection, Inc.

Stonehaven

RIVIERA ESPRIT — *Cornice-line brackets and a triple-arch entry set off a grand plan with a host of windows and outdoor places on friendly terms with sunlight.*

Balustrades, classic columns and graceful arches lend a distinctly French Beaux Arts character to this stately brick facade, set off by a sculpted window head above the two-car garage. Varied rooflines and an asymmetrical elevation create a distinctive, appealing addition to the streetscape, yet the best aspects of the home are within. A spectacular foyer opens to the spacious heart of the interior—an expansive center of planned and informal entertaining, defined only by decorative columns and ceiling treatments. Views and natural light fill the home through a wall of glass to the rear of the plan, while a retreating wall of the leisure room allows the outdoors inside. Upstairs, a wraparound loft connects the primary sleeping quarters—a magnificent master suite and a child's room and bath— with two secondary suites intended for teenagers or live-in guests.

PLAN | 8032

Bedroom: 5	Width: 58'0"
Bath: 5-1/2	Depth: 65'0"

Foundation: Slab or
   optional basement

Exterior Walls: 2x6

Main Level:	2,163 sq ft
Upper Level:	2,302 sq ft

Living Area: 4,465 sq ft

Price Code: **L2**

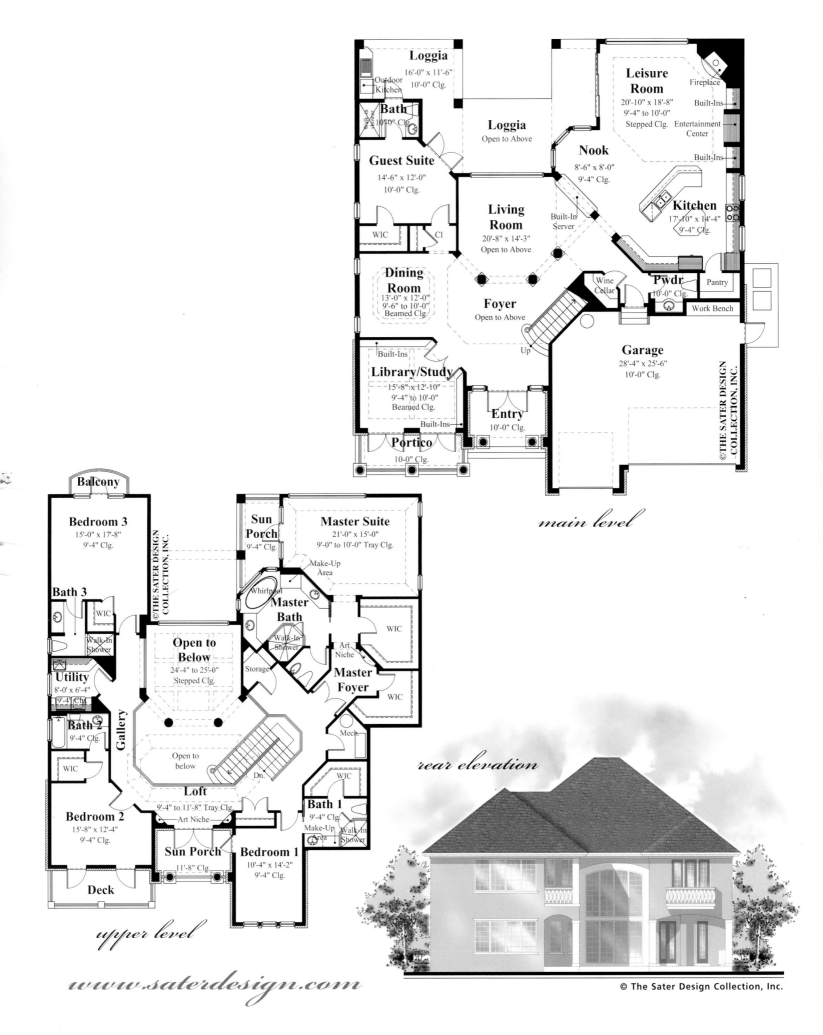

Loggia
16'-0" x 11'-6"
10'-0" Clg.

Outdoor Kitchen

Leisure Room
20'-10" x 18'-8"
9'-4" to 10'-0"
Stepped Clg.

Fireplace

Built-Ins

Entertainment Center

Built-Ins

Bath
10'-0" Clg.

Loggia
Open to Above

Nook
8'-6" x 8'-0"
9'-4" Clg.

Guest Suite
14'-6" x 12'-0"
10'-0" Clg.

Kitchen
17'-10" x 14'-4"
9'-4" Clg.

WIC

Cl

Living Room
20'-8" x 14'-3"
Open to Above

Built-In Server

Dining Room
13'-0" x 12'-0"
9'-6" to 10'-0"
Beamed Clg.

Wine Cellar

Pwdr
10'-0" Clg.

Pantry

Foyer
Open to Above

Work Bench

Built-Ins

Up

Library/Study
15'-8" x 12'-10"
9'-4" to 10'-0"
Beamed Clg.

Garage
28'-4" x 25'-6"
10'-0" Clg.

©THE SATER DESIGN COLLECTION, INC.

Built-Ins

Entry
10'-0" Clg.

Portico
10'-0" Clg.

main level

Balcony

Bedroom 3
15'-0" x 17'-8"
9'-4" Clg.

Sun Porch
9'-4" Clg.

Master Suite
21'-0" x 15'-0"
9'-0" to 10'-0" Tray Clg.

Bath 3

WIC

Make-Up Area

©THE SATER DESIGN COLLECTION, INC.

Walk In Shower

Whirlpool

Master Bath

WIC

Utility
8'-0" x 6'-4"
9'-4" Clg.

Open to Below
24'-4" to 25'-0"
Stepped Clg.

Walk-In Shower

Storage

Art Niche

Master Foyer

Gallery

Bath 2
9'-4" Clg.

WIC

Open to below

Loft
9'-4" to 11'-8" Tray Clg.

Dn.

Mech.

Bedroom 2
15'-8" x 12'-4"
9'-4" Clg.

Art Niche

Bath 1
9'-4" Clg.

WIC

Sun Porch
11'-8" Clg.

Bedroom 1
10'-4" x 14'-2"
9'-4" Clg.

Make-Up Area

Walk-In Shower

Deck

upper level

rear elevation

www.saterdesign.com

© The Sater Design Collection, Inc.

© The Sater Design Collection, Inc.

Winthrop

CONTEMPORARY HABITAT — *Innovative blends of bold, into-the-future lines and authentic renaissance details reinforce an integrated theme ready for tomorrow.*

Sculpted corbels, slump arches and parapeted dormers conceal a 21st-century interior tied to its provenance with ornate millwork, chic moldings, cornices and angled arcades. The integrity of the design is further enhanced by coffered and stepped ceiling treatments, and slender, vertical windows with transoms. A highly sophisticated arrangement of public and private rooms, though, places this plan firmly into tomorrow-like themes. At the center of the home, the living room, dining room and foyer open to one another and, when the walls retreat, extend to the wrapping rear lanai. Convenient for alfresco meals, the leisure room walls roll away, blurring the inside/outside relationship with an outdoor-kitchen area off the lanai. Authentic detailing plays in harmony with cutting-edge technology throughout the home, particularly in the kitchen, where Euro cabinetry and stainless steel culinary appliances reside together.

PLAN | *8034*

Bedroom: 3   Width: 83'10"
Bath: 4   Depth: 106'0"
Foundation: Slab
Exterior Walls: 2x6

Main Level: 3,942 sq ft

Living Area: 3,942 sq ft

Price Code: **L1**

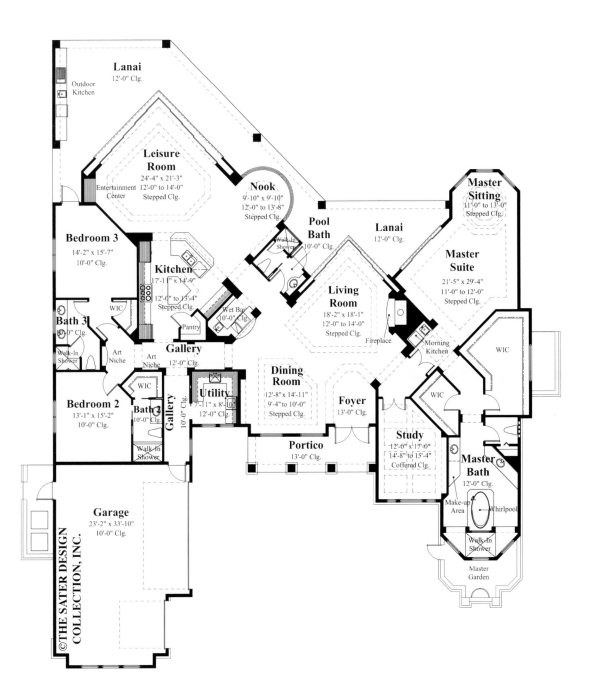

Lanai
12'-0" Clg.

Outdoor Kitchen

Leisure Room
24'-4" x 21'-3"
12'-0" to 14'-0"
Stepped Clg.

Entertainment Center

Nook
9'-10" x 9'-10"
12'-0" to 13'-8"
Stepped Clg.

Pool Bath
10'-0" Clg.

Walk-In Shower

Lanai
12'-0" Clg.

Master Sitting
11'-0" to 13'-0"
Stepped Clg.

Bedroom 3
14'-2" x 15'-7"
10'-0" Clg.

Kitchen
17'-11" x 14'-9"
12'-0" to 13'-4"
Stepped Clg.

WIC

Wet Bar
10'-0" Clg.

Living Room
18'-2" x 18'-1"
12'-0" to 14'-0"
Stepped Clg.

Master Suite
21'-5" x 29'-4"
11'-0" to 12'-0"
Stepped Clg.

WIC

Bath 3
10'-0" Clg.

Walk-In Shower

Art Niche

Pantry

Art Niche

Gallery
12'-0" Clg.

Dining Room
12'-8" x 14'-11"
9'-4" to 10'-0"
Stepped Clg.

Fireplace

Morning Kitchen

WIC

Bedroom 2
13'-1" x 15'-2"
10'-0" Clg.

Bath 2
10'-0" Clg.

Walk-In Shower

WIC

Gallery
10'-0" Clg.

Utility
7'-11" x 8'-10"
12'-0" Clg.

Foyer
13'-0" Clg.

Study
12'-0" x 17'-0"
14'-8" to 15'-4"
Coffered Clg.

Master Bath
12'-0" Clg.

Garage
23'-2" x 33'-10"
10'-0" Clg.

Portico
13'-0" Clg.

Make-up Area

Whirlpool

Walk-In Shower

Master Garden

©THE SATER DESIGN COLLECTION, INC.

rear elevation

© The Sater Design Collection, Inc.

Medoro

NATURAL BEAUTY — *Glass turrets and shingle-clad gables frame a simply elegant entry, melding 20th-century charm with an into-the-future look that's entirely down-to-earth.*

Fretwork detail, shutters and stunning bay windows embellish a subdued brick facade — influenced by the historic cottages of rural France yet definitely designed for present-day lifestyles. A sophisticated arrangement of interior spaces permits the center of the home to flex easily from private to public use. Great beamed and coffered ceilings enrich a trio of amenities shared by the great room and formal dining room: an entertainment center, built-in shelves and an extended-hearth fireplace. French doors connect the main zones with a wraparound lanai, which harbors the morning bay. Nearby, the master wing includes a cabana bath as well as a private retreat for the owners. Clustered secondary bedrooms on the upper level share a spacious deck, a compartmented bath, and a loft that leads to bonus space.

PLAN | *8039*

Bedroom: 3   Width: 72'0"

Bath: 3-1/2   Depth: 68'3"

Foundation: Slab or
    optional basement

Exterior Walls: 2x6

Main Level: 2,250 sq ft
Upper Level: 663 sq ft

Living Area: 2,913 sq ft
Bonus Room: 351 sq ft

Price Code: **C3**

Lanai
26'-0" x 15'-10"
10'-0" Clg.

Master Suite
13'-2" x 21'-2"
12'-0" to 13'-0"
Stepped Clg.

Walk-In Shower

Bath 1
10'-0" Clg.

L

Great Room
21'-3" x 17'-8"
Vaulted w/ Beamed Clg.

Fireplace

Entertainment Center

Built-In Shelves

Nook
9'-0" to 10'-0"
Stepped Clg.

Kitchen
13'-0" x 13'-9"
9'-0" to 9'-6"
Stepped Clg.

Dining Room
11'-10" x 12'-8"
9'-0" to 10'-0"
Coffered Clg.

WIC   WIC

Walk-In Shower

Master Bath
12'-0" Clg.

Whirlpool

Study
11'-0" x 15'-4"
16'-4" to 17'-4"
Beamed Clg.

Foyer
18'-8" to 19'-8"
Stepped Clg.

Dn.   Storage

Gallery
10'-0" Clg.

Pwdr.
0'-0" Clg.

Utility
6'-8" x 12'-0"
10'-0" Clg.

Entry
18'-8" Clg.

main level

Garage
21'-0" x 25'-4"
10'-0" Clg.

©THE SATER DESIGN COLLECTION, INC.

©THE SATER DESIGN COLLECTION, INC.

Deck
26'-0" x 15'-10"

Bedroom 1
13'-0" x 14'-6"
9'-4" to 10'-4"
Tray Clg.

Bedroom 2
12'-2" x 14'-4"
10'-0" Clg.

Bath 2
10'-0" Clg.

WIC

Walk-In Shower

Linen

Loft
10'-0" Clg.

Dn.   Desk   Niche

Bonus Bath
9'-8" Clg.

Walk-In Shower

upper level

Bonus Room
16'-6" x 19'-2"
Vaulted to 9'-8" Clg.

rear elevation

www.saterdesign.com

© The Sater Design Collection, Inc.

© The Sater Design Collection, Inc.

Brittany

WAY PAST COOL — *Quoins and rusticated columns shake off the past to embody a thoroughly new Euro style, with rows of splendid windows and a dash of panache.*

This enchanting villa is more than a home—it's a lifestyle. Centered flexible space serves elegant occasions yet settles down to a deeply comfortable gathering place for family and friends. A row of French doors extend the living area to the wraparound veranda, which boasts a cabana-style powder bath, an outdoor grille and plenty of space for stargazing and meals alfresco. Retreating walls in the leisure room promise a deep level of repose—and some fun movie nights at home. Sited toward the rear property, the master retreat includes dressing space, separate vanities and private access to the study. On the opposite side of the plan, a gallery hall links two secondary suites with the casual living area and kitchen— a perfect arrangement for teenagers seeking a late-night snack.

PLAN | *8040*

Bedroom: 3   Width: 84'0"

Bath: 2 Full &   Depth: 92'0"
2 Half

Foundation: Slab

Exterior Walls: 2x6

Main Level: 3,351 sq ft

Living Area: 3,351 sq ft

Price Code: **C4**

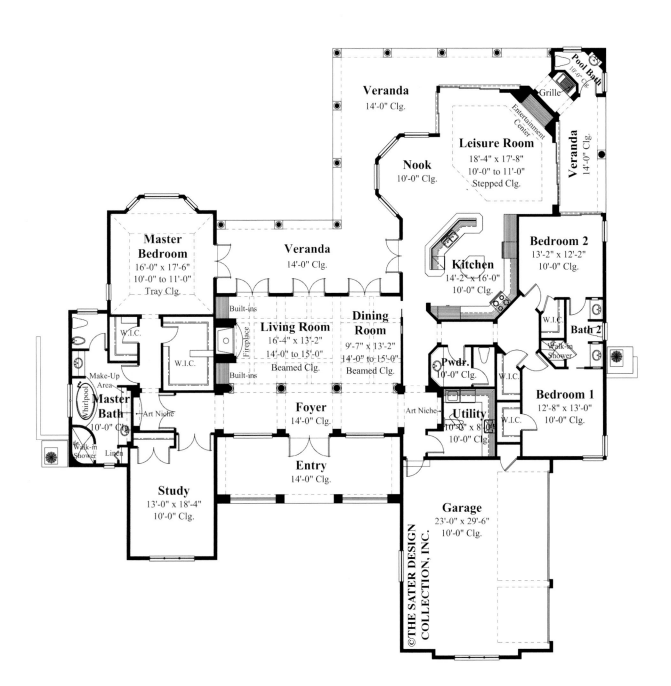

Veranda
14'-0" Clg.

Pool Bath
10'-0" Clg.

Grille

Leisure Room
18'-4" x 17'-8"
10'-0" to 11'-0"
Stepped Clg.

Nook
10'-0" Clg.

Entertainment Center

Veranda
14'-0" Clg.

Master Bedroom
16'-0" x 17'-6"
10'-0" to 11'-0"
Tray Clg.

Veranda
14'-0" Clg.

Kitchen
14'-2" x 16'-0"
10'-0" Clg.

Bedroom 2
13'-2" x 12'-2"
10'-0" Clg.

W.I.C.

W.I.C.

Fireplace

Living Room
16'-4" x 13'-2"
14'-0" to 15'-0"
Beamed Clg.

Dining Room
9'-7" x 13'-2"
14'-0" to 15'-0"
Beamed Clg.

Built-ins

Built-ins

W.I.C.

W.I.C.

Bath 2

Walk-in Shower

W.I.C.

Make-Up Area

Master Bath
10'-0" Clg.

Whirlpool

Art Niche

Foyer
14'-0" Clg.

Art Niche

Pwdr.
10'-0" Clg.

Bedroom 1
12'-8" x 13'-0"
10'-0" Clg.

W.I.C.

Utility
10'-0" x 8'
10'-0" Clg.

Walk-in Shower

Linen

Study
13'-0" x 18'-4"
10'-0" Clg.

Entry
14'-0" Clg.

Garage
23'-0" x 29'-6"
10'-0" Clg.

©THE SATER DESIGN COLLECTION, INC.

rear elevation

© The Sater Design Collection, Inc.

Beauchamp

CLASSIC CHIC — *Time-honored details pay no attention to passing trends—
fabulous architecture merely mixes the ease of luxury with the feeling of home.*

Dentils, rusticated pilasters, pediments and quoins set off a symmetrical facade
that calls up the aristocratic lines of 16th-century French renaissance villas. An
ornamented pediment and a roofline balustrade framed by two chimneys indicate
a later, Beaux Arts influence. The stunning mix of distinctive rugged stone and
smooth stucco is reiterated throughout the interior, with satisfying combinations
of timber-beamed and sleekly coffered ceilings, and rustic surrounds neighbored
by high-tech electronics. An island entertainment center provides definition and
warmth to the casual zone, separating the game room and the leisure space,
which opens to the outdoors. Positioned toward a private veranda, the guest suite
boasts a walk-in shower and compartmented vanity. An optional third family
bedroom would include a walk-in closet and hall access to the guest bath. Near
the master retreat, a cabana bath offers access to the veranda.

PLAN | *8044*

Bedroom: 4   Width: 80'8"

Bath: 3-1/2   Depth: 104'8"

Foundation: Slab or
   optional basement

Exterior Walls: 2x6

Main Level: 3,790 sq ft

Living Area: 3,790 sq ft

Price Code: **L1**

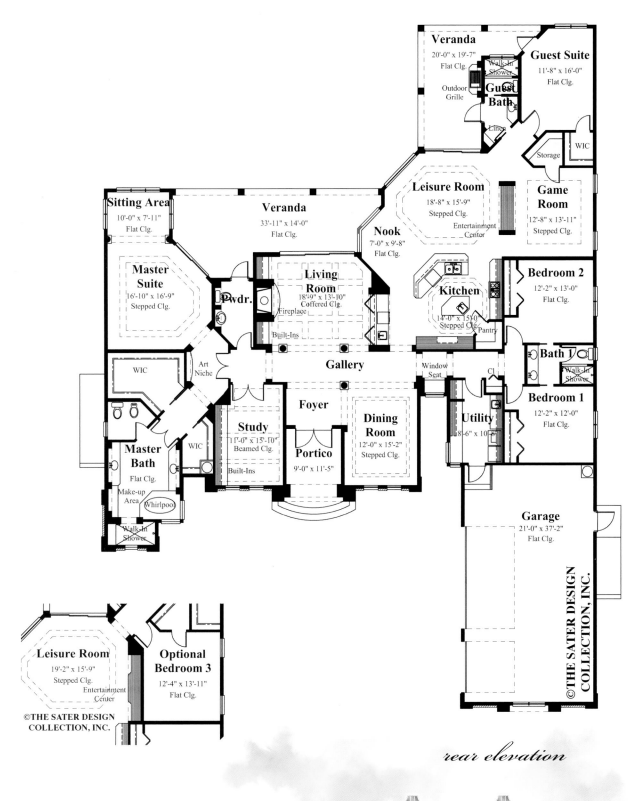

Veranda
20'-0" x 19'-7"
Flat Clg.

Outdoor Grille

Walk-In Shower

Guest Bath

Linen

Guest Suite
11'-8" x 16'-0"
Flat Clg.

WIC

Storage

Sitting Area
10'-0" x 7'-11"
Flat Clg.

Veranda
33'-11" x 14'-0"
Flat Clg.

Leisure Room
18'-8" x 15'-9"
Stepped Clg.

Entertainment Center

Game Room
12'-8" x 13'-11"
Stepped Clg.

Master Suite
16'-10" x 16'-9"
Stepped Clg.

Pwdr.

Nook
7'-0" x 9'-8"
Flat Clg.

Living Room
18'-19" x 13'-10"
Coffered Clg.

Fireplace

Built-Ins

Kitchen
14'-0" x 15'-0"
Stepped Clg.

Pantry

Bedroom 2
12'-2" x 13'-0"
Flat Clg.

WIC

Art Niche

Gallery

Window Seat

Cl.

Bath 1

Walk-In Shower

Master Bath
Flat Clg.

WIC

Study
11'-0" x 15'-10"
Beamed Clg.

Built-Ins

Foyer

Portico
9'-0" x 11'-5"

Dining Room
12'-0" x 15'-2"
Stepped Clg.

Utility
8'-6" x 10'

Bedroom 1
12'-2" x 12'-0"
Flat Clg.

Make-up Area

Whirlpool

Walk-In Shower

Garage
21'-0" x 37'-2"
Flat Clg.

©THE SATER DESIGN COLLECTION, INC.

Leisure Room
19'-2" x 15'-9"
Stepped Clg.

Entertainment Center

Optional Bedroom 3
12'-4" x 13'-11"
Flat Clg.

©THE SATER DESIGN COLLECTION, INC.

rear elevation

www.saterdesign.com

© The Sater Design Collection, Inc.

© The Sater Design Collection, Inc.

Solaine

LA BELLE EPOQUE — *Classy and chic, with fashionable curves in all the right places, this French manor calls up gentler times yet conceals a smart interior.*

Rusticated columns and a balcony balustrade on this stately elevation suggest early 20th-century influences, yet the spacious interior is purely today. The portico yields to an open foyer that is defined by tapered columns and graceful arches. Well-defined formal rooms flank the gallery that leads to the great room. Three sets of French doors invite a sense of nature within, and link the space to an outdoor room: a patio terrace suited for stargazing or open air dining. Nearby, a splendid loggia boasts an outdoor grille and a link to the morning nook and kitchen. The right wing of the home is dedicated to the owners' retreat, with a sitting area in the bedroom brightened by a bow window. On the upper level, a gallery loft permits views of the great room below, and links four secondary bedrooms—one with private access to a sun deck.

PLAN	*8051*

Bedroom: 5   Width: 72'0"
Bath: 3-1/2   Depth: 71'0"
Foundation: Slab
Exterior Walls: 2x6

Main Level: 2,163 sq ft
Upper Level: 1,415 sq ft

Living Area: 3,578 sq ft

Price Code: **L1**

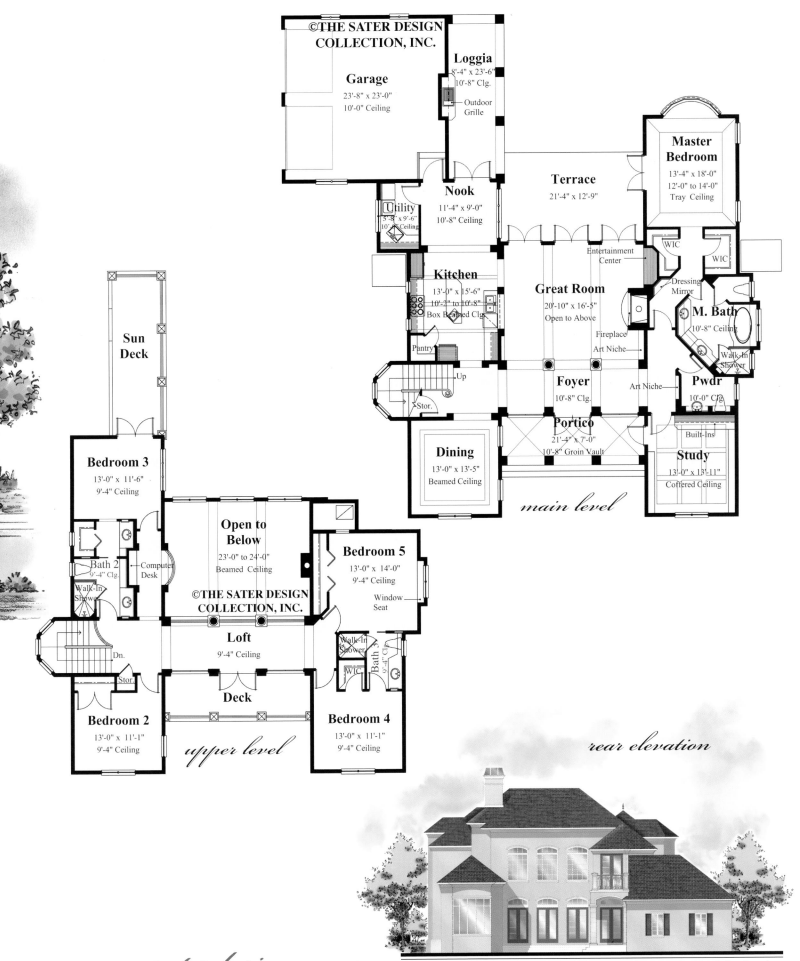

©THE SATER DESIGN COLLECTION, INC.

Garage
23'-8" x 23'-0"
10'-0" Ceiling

Loggia
8'-4" x 23'-6"
10'-8" Clg.

Outdoor Grille

Nook
11'-4" x 9'-0"
10'-8" Ceiling

Terrace
21'-4" x 12'-9"

Master Bedroom
13'-4" x 18'-0"
12'-0" to 14'-0"
Tray Ceiling

Utility
5'-8" x 9'-6"
10' Ceiling

WIC

WIC

Kitchen
13'-0" x 15'-6"
10'-2" to 10'-8"
Box Beamed Clg.

Entertainment Center

Great Room
20'-10" x 16'-5"
Open to Above

Dressing Mirror

M. Bath
10'-8" Ceiling

Pantry

Fireplace

Art Niche

Walk-In Shower

Up

Stor.

Foyer
10'-8" Clg.

Art Niche

Pwdr
10'-0" Clg.

Dining
13'-0" x 13'-5"
Beamed Ceiling

Portico
21'-4" x 7'-0"
10'-8" Groin Vault

Built-Ins

Study
13'-0" x 13'-11"
Coffered Ceiling

main level

Sun Deck

Bedroom 3
13'-0" x 11'-6"
9'-4" Ceiling

Open to Below
23'-0" to 24'-0"
Beamed Ceiling

©THE SATER DESIGN COLLECTION, INC.

Bedroom 5
13'-0" x 14'-0"
9'-4" Ceiling

Bath 2
9'-4" Clg.

Computer Desk

Window Seat

Walk-In Shower

Walk-In Shower

Loft
9'-4" Ceiling

Dn.

Stor.

WIC

Bath 3
9'-4" Clg.

Deck

Bedroom 2
13'-0" x 11'-1"
9'-4" Ceiling

upper level

Bedroom 4
13'-0" x 11'-1"
9'-4" Ceiling

rear elevation

www.saterdesign.com

© The Sater Design Collection, Inc.

© The Sater Design Collection, Inc.

Christabel

JOY HOUSE — *The liberating inside/outside spaces of this native French plan invite the kind of repose one might find on a beach on the Riviera.*

Charming accents of stacked stone and wood shutters lend rural elements to this urbane design. A glass-paneled door leads to an interior that offers open-air vistas from every room of the house. Rustic and relaxed, the rooms connect with nature in elemental ways: the use of natural materials, a sense of human scale and lines, and dissolving the boundaries with the great outdoors. To the rear of the plan, a rambling lanai offers a daily invitation to linger beneath a tranquil shelter from the sun. A refined arrangement of the forward rooms plays counterpoint to the wide-open, into-the-future casual zone, which boasts a wall-sized entertainment center. Retreating walls grant access to the lanai and, on the side of the plan, a courtyard warmed by a massive masonry fireplace. Craftsmanship creates texture throughout the home, while sleek columns and glass walls provide a subdued backdrop.

PLAN | *8053*

Bedroom: 4   Width: 74'8"
Bath: 3-1/2   Depth: 118'0"
Foundation: Slab
Exterior Walls: 2x6

Main Level: 2,974 sq ft
Guest Suite: 297 sq ft
_____

Living Area: 3,271 sq ft

Price Code: **C4**

Guest Suite
13'-0" x 16'-2"
10'-0" Clg.

Lanai
28'-8" x 27'-0"
10'-8" Clg.

Walk-In Shower

Guest Bath
10'-0" Clg.

Outdoor Grille

Master Suite
13'-4" x 20'-8"
10'-0" to 11'-0"
Stepped Clg.

Leisure Room
20'-6" x 18'-6"
10'-8" to 11'-8"
Coffered Clg.

Entertainment Center

WIC   WIC

Lanai
17'-0" x 12'-11"
10'-8" Clg.

Nook
10'-0" x 11'-5"
10'-8" Clg.

Lanai
11'-3" x 46'-0"
10'-8" Clg.

Fireplace

Kitchen
18'-0" x 15'-3"
10'-8" Clg.

Art Niche

Art Niche

Wet Bar

Pantry

WIC

Bedroom 2
12'-0" x 12'-6"
10'-0" Clg.

M. Bath
10'-0" Clg.

Whirlpool

Living Room
11'-6" x 14'-4"
12'-4" to 13'-4"
Coffered Clg.

Foyer
13'-4" Clg.

Dining
11'-8" x 14'-4"
12'-4" to 13'-4"
Stepped Clg.

Pwdr.
10'-0" Clg.

Linen

Walk-In Shower

Entry
13'-4" Clg.

Bath 2
10'-0" Clg.

Utility
8'-6" x 8'-0"
10'-0" Clg.

WIC

Bedroom 3
13'-6" x 14'-10"
10'-0" Clg.

Garage
23'-0" x 30'-10"
11'-4" Clg.

©THE SATER DESIGN COLLECTION, INC.

rear elevation

www.saterdesign.com

© The Sater Design Collection, Inc.

Argentellas

NEW PERSPECTIVE — *Glimpses of a facade that's a little bit French Country, and a little bit European romantic.*

Classic dormers and a graceful colonnade live in harmony with stately turrets and staggered rooflines with this modern elevation. Surprises prevail throughout the interior, with nature intruding on the formal rooms, and outdoor areas that beckon from even intimate spaces. The entry portico leads into the home through a trio of glass-paneled doors; inside, a gallery foyer links two private wings and grants panoramic views through the rear of the plan. A wrapping veranda provides an outdoor grille for dining alfresco, plus shelter from the sun. The made-for-the-future gourmet kitchen is a culinary paradise, with two food-prep islands—one with a veggie sink—and a corner walk-in pantry, near the six-burner stove. To the right of the main level, the master wing offers a place of respite for very busy owners.

PLAN | *8056*

Bedroom: 5	Width: 69'4"
Bath: 4-1/2	Depth: 95'4"

Foundation: Slab or
  optional basement

Exterior Walls: 2x6

Main Level:	2,920 sq ft
Upper Level:	1,478 sq ft

Living Area: 4,398 sq ft

Price Code: **L2**

Pool Bath
Outdoor Grille

Veranda
29'-9" x 25'-4" Avg.
10'-0" Clg.

Leisure Room
20'-4" x 17'-4"
9'-4" to 10'-0"
Stepped Clg.

Built-In Entertainment

Nook
9'-4" Clg.

Veranda
8'-8" x 18'-2"
14'-2" Clg.

Master Suite
15'-0" x 21'-6"
12'-0" to 13'-0"
Stepped Ceiling

Kitchen
13'-8" x 14'-8"
9'-4" to 10'-0"
Stepped Clg.

Courtyard

Dining Room
10'-0" x 14'-2"
9'-0" to 10'-0"
Stepped Clg.

Living Room
18'-2" x 14'-2"
Open to Above

Fireplace

WIC

WIC

Pantry

Study/ Bedroom 5
12'-2" x 13'-8"
10'-0" Clg.

Bath 1
10'-0" Clg.

Laundry Chute

Foyer
16'-0" Clg.

Art Niche

Opt. Closet   Storage

Walk-In Shower

Family Valet

Wine Cellar

Up

Portico
18'-8" x 7'-3"
13'-4" Clg.

Master Bath
12'-8" to 12'-8"
Stepped Clg.

Whirlpool

Coat Closet

Walk-In Shower

Utility
8'-2" x 6'-0"
10'-0" Clg.

main level

© THE SATER DESIGN COLLECTION, INC.

Garage
23'-0" x 31'-2"
10'-0" Clg.

©THE SATER DESIGN COLLECTION, INC.

Deck
35'-1" x 8'-0"

Walk-In Shower

Bedroom 2
14'-0" x 13'-0"
9'-4" Clg.

Bath 2
9'-4" Clg.

Bedroom 1
13'-5" x 13'-10"
9'-4" Clg.

WIC

WIC

Bedroom 3
16'-2" x 12'-0"
9'-4" Clg.

Bath 3
9'-4" Clg.

WIC

Loft
10'-10" x 13'-8"
9'-4" Clg.

Open to Below
18'-4" x 19'-4"
Vaulted Clg.

Bedroom 4
12'-4" x 14'-0"
9'-4" Clg.

WIC

Linen

Laundry Chute

Storage Room

Dn.

Open to Below

upper level

rear elevation

www.saterdesign.com

© The Sater Design Collection, Inc.

© The Sater Design Collection, Inc.

Le Marescott

ESPRIT DE FRANCE — *Hipped rooflines confirm the traditional character of this neo-Norman elevation, yet walls toned in Mango imply a twist in the vernacular.*

A flared eave sets a very French tone for this facade, designed to lend an established presence to the neighborhood. An interior of intimate spaces, angled walls and open rooms melds razor's-edge technology with a sense of nature— old-world charm with smart Euro functions. Classic columns are toe-to-toe with zesty metal appliances; retreating walls bring richly carved cabinetry in touch with the great outdoors. A beamed ceiling highlights the study—a flex space that converts to guest quarters, a movie room or even a nursery—and back again. The gourmet kitchen is well equipped for the most sophisticated events, but this culinary paradise can also whip up a peanut butter and jelly sandwich with quick trips from the lanai. French doors link the owners' retreat with an outside sitting area that boasts a grille. Spacious guest quarters provide a cabana-style bath and punctuate a cluster of family bedrooms. A family valet, conveniently located, provides the perfect place to drop your keys and packages.

PLAN | *8060*

Bedroom: 4   Width: 67'0"
Bath: 3-1/2   Depth: 90'8"
Foundation: Slab
Exterior Walls: 8" CBS or 2x6

Main Level: 3,246 sq ft

Living Area: 3,246 sq ft

Price Code: **C4**

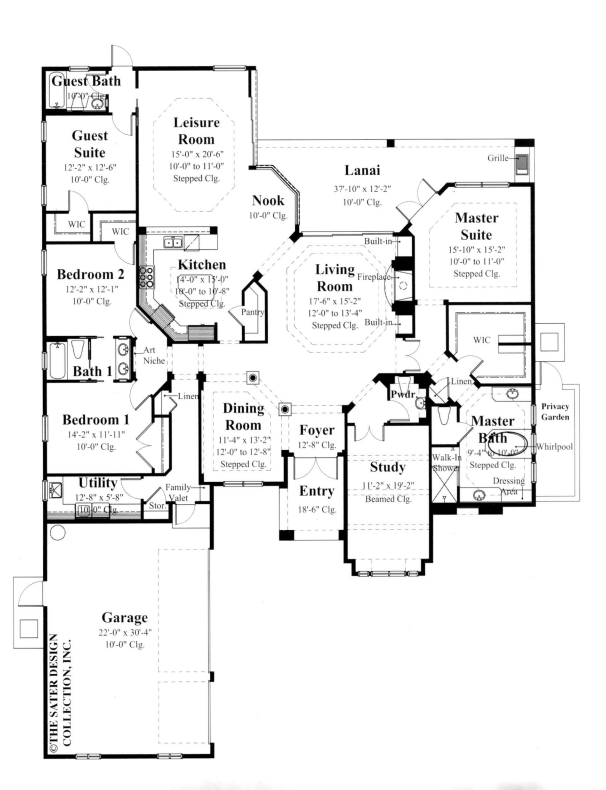

Guest Bath
10'-0" Clg.

Guest Suite
12'-2" x 12'-6"
10'-0" Clg.

Leisure Room
15'-0" x 20'-6"
10'-0" to 11'-0"
Stepped Clg.

Lanai
37'-10" x 12'-2"
10'-0" Clg.

Grille

WIC

WIC

Nook
10'-0" Clg.

Master Suite
15'-10" x 15'-2"
10'-0" to 11'-0"
Stepped Clg.

Built-in

Bedroom 2
12'-2" x 12'-1"
10'-0" Clg.

Kitchen
14'-0" x 13'-0"
10'-0" to 10'-8"
Stepped Clg.

Living Room
17'-6" x 15'-2"
12'-0" to 13'-4"
Stepped Clg.

Fireplace

Pantry

Built-in

WIC

Art Niche

Bath 1

Linen

Linen

Pwdr.

Master Bath
9'-4" to 10'-0"
Stepped Clg.

Privacy Garden

Whirlpool

Bedroom 1
14'-2" x 11'-11"
10'-0" Clg.

Dining Room
11'-4" x 13'-2"
12'-0" to 12'-8"
Stepped Clg.

Foyer
12'-8" Clg.

Study
11'-2" x 19'-2"
Beamed Clg.

Walk-In Shower

Dressing Area

Utility
12'-8" x 5'-8"
10'-0" Clg.

Family Valet

Stor.

Entry
18'-6" Clg.

Garage
22'-0" x 30'-4"
10'-0" Clg.

©THE SATER DESIGN COLLECTION, INC.

rear elevation

www.saterdesign.com

© The Sater Design Collection, Inc.

© The Sater Design Collection, Inc.

Fontana

IN VOGUE — *Fanlight transoms set off a fundamental chic that subdues the streetscape and speaks to the future in a dialect of its own.*

Copper arched dormers echo the graceful curves of a circular window, taking on an eclectic French facade of powerful colonial forms. The recessed entry harbors a paneled door, which leads to an open foyer. Oriented toward views to the rear of the home, the plan allows spectacular vistas, even from the front door. Tapered columns and a wall of glass define the living room, which hosts an extended-hearth fireplace framed by built-in cabinetry. Stepped ceilings offer a subtle sense of separation of space in an open arrangement of the formal rooms. To the left of the plan, a cabana-style powder bath serves the pool area and maintains privacy for the master wing. The owners' retreat sports a sitting area, a walk-in closet designed for two, a shoe wardrobe, and a luxe bath with separate everything. A family valet, conveniently located, provides the perfect place to drop your keys and packages.

PLAN | *8062*

Bedroom: 4   Width: 68'8"
Bath: 3-1/2   Depth: 91'8"
Foundation: Slab
Exterior Walls: 2x6

Main Level: 3,497 sq ft

Living Area: 3,497 sq ft

Price Code: **C4**

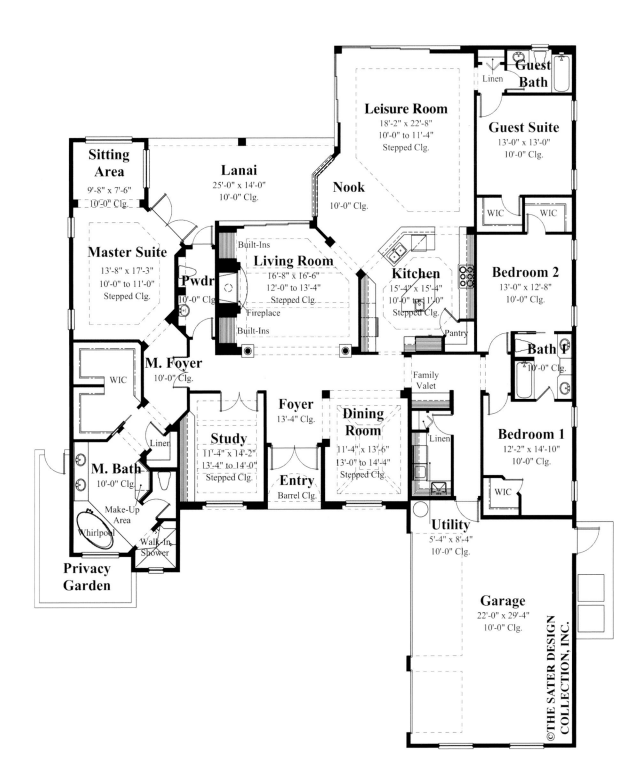

Guest Bath

Linen

Leisure Room
18'-2" x 22'-8"
10'-0" to 11'-4"
Stepped Clg.

Guest Suite
13'-0" x 13'-0"
10'-0" Clg.

Sitting Area
9'-8" x 7'-6"
10'-0" Clg.

Lanai
25'-0" x 14'-0"
10'-0" Clg.

Nook
10'-0" Clg.

WIC

WIC

Master Suite
13'-8" x 17'-3"
10'-0" to 11'-0"
Stepped Clg.

Pwdr
10'-0" Clg.

Living Room
16'-8" x 16'-6"
12'-0" to 13'-4"
Stepped Clg.

Built-Ins

Built-Ins

Fireplace

Kitchen
15'-4" x 15'-4"
10'-0" to 11'-0"
Stepped Clg.

Bedroom 2
13'-0" x 12'-8"
10'-0" Clg.

Pantry

WIC

M. Foyer
10'-0" Clg.

Liner

Family Valet

Bath
10'-0" Clg.

Foyer
13'-4" Clg.

Study
11'-4" x 14'-2"
13'-4" to 14'-0"
Stepped Clg.

Dining Room
11'-4" x 13'-6"
13'-0" to 14'-4"
Stepped Clg.

Linen

Bedroom 1
12'-2" x 14'-10"
10'-0" Clg.

M. Bath
10'-0" Clg.

Entry
Barrel Clg.

WIC

Make-Up Area

Whirlpool

Walk In Shower

Utility
5'-4" x 8'-4"
10'-0" Clg.

Privacy Garden

Garage
22'-0" x 29'-4"
10'-0" Clg.

©THE SATER DESIGN COLLECTION, INC.

rear elevation

© The Sater Design Collection, Inc.

Bartlett

COUNTRY FLAVOR — *A rural vocabulary of curvy balusters and symmetrical stone evokes the quiet charm of French country houses with this up-to-date plan.*

Hipped rooflines and a triplet of dormers provide chic contrast to sculpted aspects of this Euro elevation: hips, turrets and an entry loggia. The paneled front door offers a thoroughfare for fresh breezes, and perhaps the scent of pinon trees and ocean. Interior vistas that extend beyond the walls of glass to the rear of the plan dominate the grand foyer and central living room. Along the gallery, a series of tapered columns and soffits maximize the effects of an open-room scale, drawing light even into the forward rooms. A slow-down, shoes-off atmosphere prevails in the casual living zone, with a bay of French doors that allow nature to intrude on a vibrant arrangement of rooms. Well positioned to access the leisure space, morning nook, formal dining room and outdoor eating area, the kitchen serves many occasions with ease.

PLAN | *8064*

Bedroom: 4   Width: 95'0"
Bath: 3-1/2   Depth: 82'8"
Foundation: Slab or
    optional basement
Exterior Walls: 2x6

Main Level: 3,588 sq ft
Upper Level: 1,287 sq ft

Living Area: 4,875 sq ft

Price Code: **L2**

Verandah
31'-2" x 19'-8"
12'-6" Clg.

Leisure Room
16'-2" x 25'-2"
12'-0" to 13'-4" Clg.

Nook
10'-0" to 12'-0" Clg.

Verandah
37'-0" x 12'-4"
10'-6" Clg.

Master Suite
17'-0" x 21'-1"
12'-0" to 14'-0"
Stepped Clg.

Kitchen
16'-1" x 21'-8"
9'-4" Clg.

Living Room
18'-2" x 19'-2"
Open to Above

Study
11'-6" x 14'-6"
10'-0" Clg.

Utility
11'-6" x 8'-0"
10'-0" Clg.

Stor.

2-Sided Fireplace

Built-Ins

WIC
6'-7" x 8'-8"

WIC
5'-0" x 14'-6"

Desk

Pantry

Art Niche

Gallery

Foyer

Gallery

Art Niche

Stor.

Linen

Pwdr.
10'-0" Clg.

Dining
14'-8" x 16'-4"
10'-0" Clg.

Entry

Up

Walk-In Shower

Garage
22'-4" x 34'-8"
11'-8" Clg.

Master Bath
Vaulted Clg.

©THE SATER DESIGN COLLECTION, INC.

Whirlpool Tub

main level

Balcony
12'-6" x 12'-4"

©THE SATER DESIGN COLLECTION, INC.

Balcony
16'-6" x 12'-4"

WIC

Bedroom 2
14'-11" x 16'-0"
9'-0" Clg.

Open to Below
Coffered Clg.

Bedroom 3
13'-0" x 14'-6"
9'-0" Clg.

Walk-In Shower

Walk-In Shower

Bath 2
9'-0" Clg.

WIC

Bath 3
9'-0" Clg.

Linen

WIC

Balcony
9'-0" Clg.

Bedroom 4
14'-8" x 16'-4"
9'-0" Clg.

Balcony
18'-8" x 5'-8"

Dn.

upper level

rear elevation

Photograph by: Kim Sargent

REGION/STYLE | *English*

Country, Cotswold, Gothic, Revival and Rural—

a new breed of design interprets the past in ways that are formal and

sophisticated yet also friendly and livable.

Craftsmanship and a spirit of refinement are key to these houses,

with sculpted arcades,

breezy porches and rambling terraces—

designed to step into the future.

© The Sater Design Collection, Inc.

Clarissant

PERFECT MATCH — *Elizabethan lines and rugged Cotswold textures promote sensibilities of both comfort and style, with the intimacy of a country cottage.*

Two-story bays, a renaissance entry and overlapping gables enhance the high-glam presentation of this English-inspired manor. Exposed eave brackets and peek-a-boo dormers establish a rural style that is definitely grand, yet a modest introduction to a splendid interior designed for sophisticated lifestyles. The forward plan integrates a pleasing palette of colors and textures with out-of-this-world amenities and spectacular interior vistas granted by French doors and a bow window. A gallery links the grand foyer with the formal rooms, including a private study, an open formal dining room and a palatial living room that leads outdoors. Built-ins and a massive fireplace anchor the leisure space, which boasts a wall of glass shared with the morning nook, and easy access to the veranda. Upper-level sleeping quarters are connected by a balcony hall that overlooks the foyer and living room.

PLAN | *8002*

Bedroom: 4   Width: 85'0"

Bath: 3-1/2   Depth: 76'7"

Foundation: Slab or
    optional basement

Exterior Walls: 2x6

Main Level: 2,794 sq ft

Upper Level: 1,152 sq ft

Living Area: 3,946 sq ft

Price Code: **L1**

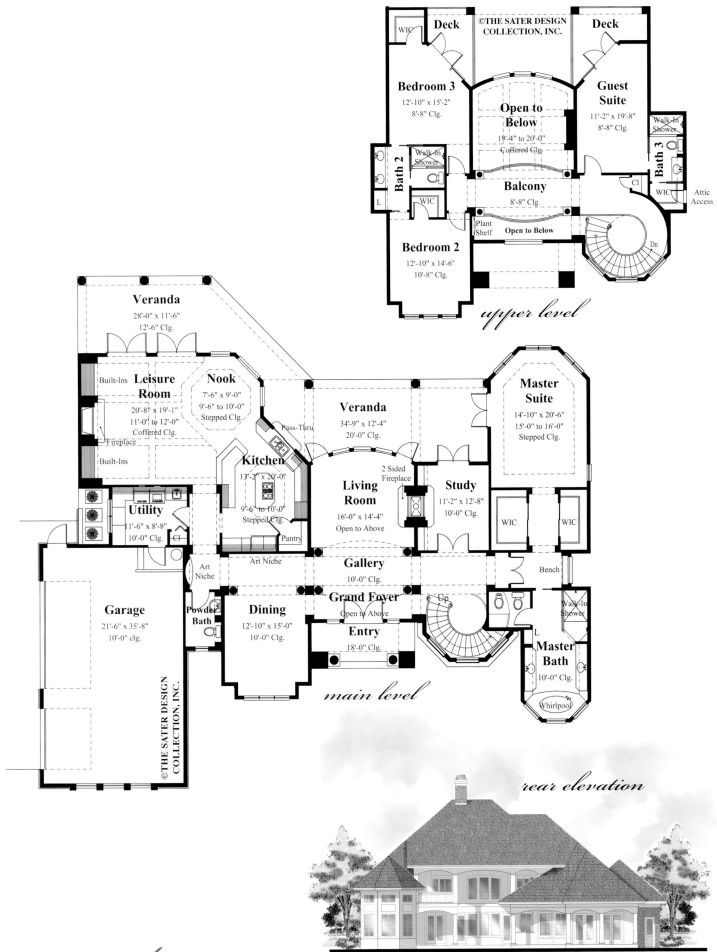

Upper Level

©THE SATER DESIGN COLLECTION, INC.

WIC

Deck

Deck

Bedroom 3
12'-10" x 15'-2"
8'-8" Clg.

Open to Below
19'-4" to 20'-0"
Coffered Clg.

Guest Suite
11'-2" x 19'-8"
8'-8" Clg.

Walk-In Shower

Bath 2

Walk-In Shower

Balcony
8'-8" Clg.

Cl

Bath 3

WIC

Attic Access

Plant Shelf

Open to Below

Dn

Bedroom 2
12'-10" x 14'-6"
10'-8" Clg.

upper level

Main Level

Veranda
28'-0" x 11'-6"
12'-6" Clg.

Built-Ins

Leisure Room
20'-8" x 19'-1"
11'-0" to 12'-0"
Coffered Clg.

Fireplace

Built-Ins

Nook
7'-6" x 9'-0"
9'-6" to 10'-0"
Stepped Clg.

Pass-Thru

Master Suite
14'-10" x 20'-6"
15'-0" to 16'-0"
Stepped Clg.

Veranda
34'-9" x 12'-4"
20'-0" Clg.

Utility
11'-6" x 8'-8"
10'-0" Clg.

Cl

Kitchen
13'-2" x 20'-0"
9'-6" to 10'-0"
Stepped Clg.

Pantry

Living Room
16'-0" x 14'-4"
Open to Above

2 Sided Fireplace

Study
11'-2" x 12'-8"
10'-0" Clg.

WIC

WIC

Art Niche

Art Niche

Gallery
10'-0" Clg.

Bench

Garage
21'-6" x 35'-8"
10'-0" clg.

Powder Bath

Dining
12'-10" x 15'-0"
10'-0" Clg.

Grand Foyer
Open to Above

Entry
18'-0" Clg.

Up

Walk-In Shower

L

Master Bath
10'-0" Clg.

Whirlpool

©THE SATER DESIGN COLLECTION, INC.

main level

rear elevation

© The Sater Design Collection, Inc.

www.saterdesign.com

© The Sater Design Collection, Inc.

Berkley

AT HOME IN THE COUNTRY — *Linen-white stucco contrasts with rugged stone on this classic country manor, evoking an elegant 19th-century theme—inside, a comfy atmosphere prevails.*

Pedimented gables, carved balusters and painted shutters call up a gentler time with this refined elevation, while a wide-open interior emphasizes the benefits of a warm climate. Many of the British styles drawn from post-Victorian country houses seek the right mix of comfort and style — this home revives that spirit of relaxed formality, with flexible spaces and wide-open views. Intentionally informal and cottage-like on the outside, the core of the plan reveals an exuberant array of round columns, graceful arches and sculpted architectural furnishings. Bay windows punctuate the formal and casual zones, letting in light and a sense of the great outdoors. Upstairs, a computer loft overlooks the great room and links the secondary bedrooms and guest quarters. A side staircase leads up to a bonus room above the garage.

PLAN | *8006*

Bedroom: 4   Width: 91'0"

Bath: 3-1/2   Depth: 52'8"

Foundation: Slab or
    optional basement

Exterior Walls: 2x6

Main Level: 2,219 sq ft

Upper Level: 1,085 sq ft

Living Area: 3,304 sq ft

Bonus Room: 404 sq ft

Price Code: **C4**

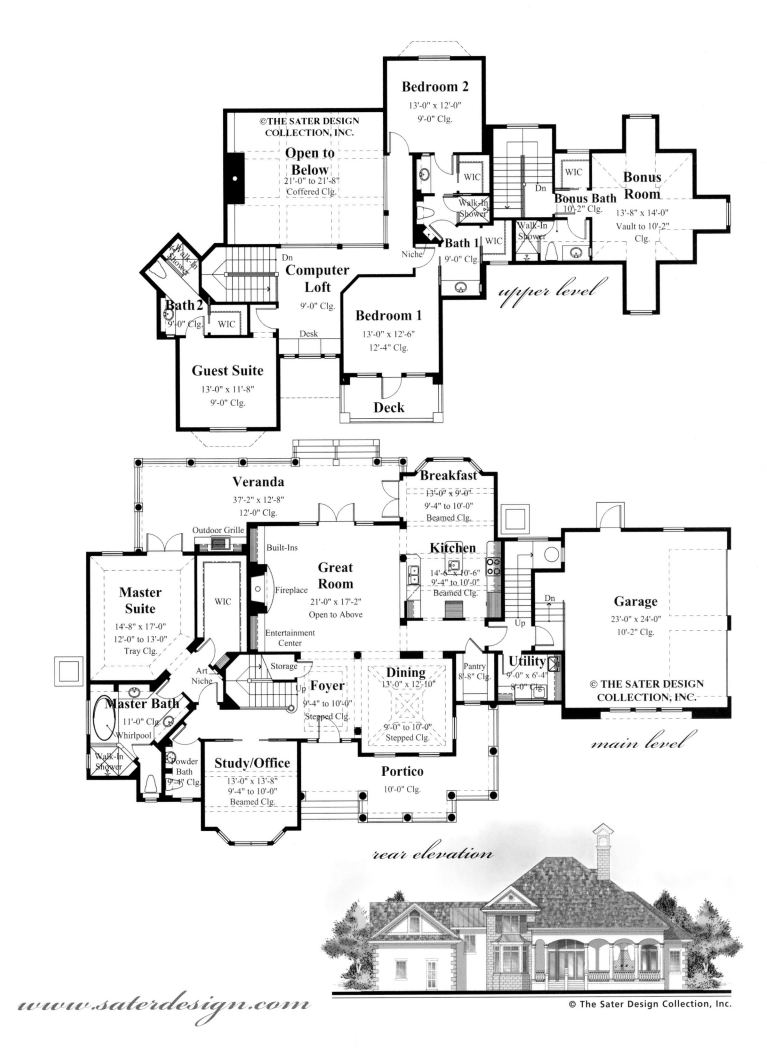

©THE SATER DESIGN COLLECTION, INC.

Bedroom 2
13'-0" x 12'-0"
9'-0" Clg.

Open to Below
21'-0" to 21'-8"
Coffered Clg.

WIC

WIC

Bonus Room
13'-8" x 14'-0"
Vault to 10'-2" Clg.

Walk-In Shower

Walk-In Shower

Bonus Bath
10'-2" Clg.

Dn

Bath 1
9'-0" Clg.

WIC

Niche

Dn

Computer Loft
9'-0" Clg.

Walk-In Shower

Bath 2
9'-0" Clg.

WIC

Desk

Bedroom 1
13'-0" x 12'-6"
12'-4" Clg.

upper level

Guest Suite
13'-0" x 11'-8"
9'-0" Clg.

Desk

Deck

Veranda
37'-2" x 12'-8"
12'-0" Clg.

Breakfast
13'-0" x 9'-0"
9'-4" to 10'-0"
Beamed Clg.

Outdoor Grille

Built-Ins

Kitchen
14'-6" x 10'-6"
9'-4" to 10'-0"
Beamed Clg.

Great Room
21'-0" x 17'-2"
Open to Above

Fireplace

Master Suite
14'-8" x 17'-0"
12'-0" to 13'-0"
Tray Clg.

WIC

Entertainment Center

Up

Dn

Garage
23'-0" x 24'-0"
10'-2" Clg.

© THE SATER DESIGN COLLECTION, INC.

Art Niche

Storage

Foyer
9'-4" to 10'-0"
Stepped Clg.

Up

Dining
13'-0" x 12'-10"
9'-0" to 10'-0"
Stepped Clg.

Pantry
8'-8" Clg.

Utility
9'-0" x 6'-4"
8'-0" Clg.

Master Bath
11'-0" Clg.

Whirlpool

Walk-In Shower

Powder Bath
9'-4" Clg.

Study/Office
13'-0" x 13'-8"
9'-4" to 10'-0"
Beamed Clg.

Portico
10'-0" Clg.

main level

rear elevation

www.saterdesign.com

© The Sater Design Collection, Inc.

© The Sater Design Collection, Inc.

New Abby

TWIST ON TRADITION — *Contemporary lines meld classic British forms with a new aesthetic — rich and refined, bold and well-crafted — a new notion of home.*

Stone and stucco create an idyllic presence with this Euro-American design—perfect for brand-new neighborhoods or established townships. A bold pediment supported by massive square columns announces the grand entry—a glass-paneled, double-leaf door flanked by decorative panels. Inside, the private and public realms are arranged laterally in order to achieve a sensible flow and practical function. Stepped ceilings, angled lines and arched passages unify the central space—three unique rooms that share an orientation to the rear of the plan, allowing great views. A secluded master wing features a spectacular bedroom with retreating walls, which open to the veranda, and a rambling bath that overlooks a private garden. The opposing side of the plan harbors the informal zone, with a well-organized kitchen, an inside/outside leisure room, and a gallery that leads to guest suites or family bedrooms.

PLAN	*8008*

Bedroom: 3   Width: 106'4"

Bath: 3-1/2   Depth: 102'4"

Foundation: Slab or
   optional basement

Exterior Walls: 2x6

Main Level: 3,640 sq ft
_____

Living Area: 3,640 sq ft

Price Code: **L1**

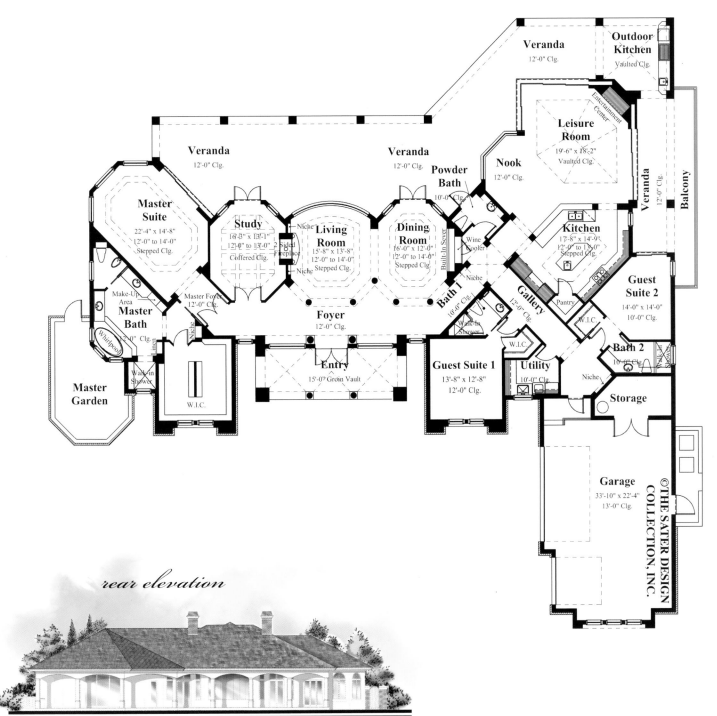

Veranda
12'-0" Clg.

Outdoor Kitchen
Vaulted Clg.

Veranda
12'-0" Clg.

Veranda
12'-0" Clg.

Leisure Room
19'-6" x 18'-2"
Vaulted Clg.

Master Suite
22'-4" x 14'-8"
12'-0" to 14'-0"
Stepped Clg.

Study
16'-3" x 13'-1"
12'-0" to 13'-0"
Coffered Clg.

Living Room
15'-8" x 13'-8"
12'-0" to 14'-0"
Stepped Clg.

Dining Room
16'-0" x 12'-0"
12'-0" to 14'-0"
Stepped Clg.

Powder Bath
10'-0" Clg.

Nook
12'-0" Clg.

Kitchen
17'-8" x 14'-9"
12'-0" to 13'-0"
Stepped Clg.

Guest Suite 2
14'-0" x 14'-0"
10'-0" Clg.

Master Bath
12'-0" Clg.

Make-Up Area

Master Foyer
12'-0" Clg.

Foyer
12'-0" Clg.

Niche

2 Sided Fireplace

Built-In Server

Wine Cooler

Bath 1
10'-0" Clg.

Gallery
12'-0" Clg.

Pantry

W.I.C.

Bath 2
10'-0" Clg.

Master Garden

Whirlpool

Walk-In Shower

W.I.C.

Linen

Entry
15'-0" Groin Vault

Walk-In Shower

W.I.C.

Guest Suite 1
13'-8" x 12'-8"
12'-0" Clg.

Utility
10'-0" Clg.

Niche

Storage

Garage
33'-10" x 22'-4"
13'-0" Clg.

©THE SATER DESIGN COLLECTION, INC.

rear elevation

© The Sater Design Collection, Inc.

walkout basement

© The Sater Design Collection, Inc.

www.saterdesign.com

© The Sater Design Collection, Inc.

Elise

GENTEEL COUNTRY — *Saturated hues and a sculpted recessed entry set off this into-the-future facade—rich with historic details and intimately linked with nature.*

Sunshine yellow and cream-white stucco surrounds a sophisticated interior of wide-open spaces and well-defined rooms. Floor-to-ceiling bow and bay windows to the rear of the plan add natural light and a sense of the outdoors to the entire heart of the home: the living room, gallery, dining room, stair hall and foyer. A lavish master retreat dominates the right wing of the main level. With a garden bath, spacious dressing area and a private sitting area, the suite displays many qualities of luxury. Textured ceilings, ornamented windows and classic embell-ishments—such as arched columns and built-ins—define the forward rooms and play counterpoint to a more subtle architecture to the rear of the plan. An airy indoor/outdoor relationship is prevalent in the shared space of the leisure room, morning nook and kitchen. On the upper level, a balcony hall enjoys vistas of the formal spaces, and links to a computer loft near the secondary bedrooms.

PLAN | 8012

Bedroom: 4   Width: 71'6"

Bath: 4-1/2   Depth: 82'2"

Foundation: Slab or optional basement

Exterior Walls: 2x6

Main Level: 2,867 sq ft

Upper Level: 1,155 sq ft

Living Area: 4,022 sq ft

Bonus Room: 371 sq ft

Price Code: **L2**

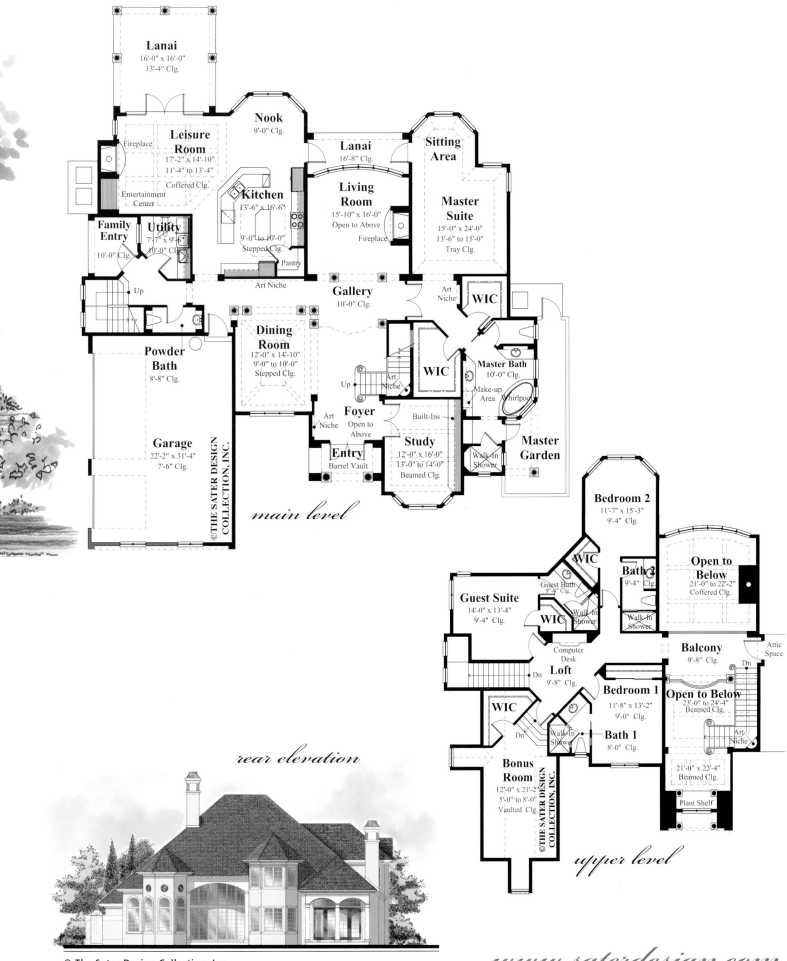

Lanai
16'-0" x 16'-0"
13'-4" Clg.

Leisure Room
17'-2" x 14'-10"
11'-4" to 13'-4"
Coffered Clg.

Fireplace

Nook
9'-0" Clg.

Lanai
16'-8" Clg.

Sitting Area

Kitchen
13'-6" x 16'-6"
9'-0" to 10'-0"
Stepped Clg.

Entertainment Center

Living Room
15'-10" x 16'-0"
Open to Above
Fireplace

Master Suite
15'-0" x 24'-0"
13'-6" to 15'-0"
Tray Clg.

Family Entry
10'-0" Clg.

Utility
7'-7" x 9'-6"
10'-0" Clg.

Pantry

Art Niche

Gallery
10'-0" Clg.

Art Niche

WIC

Powder Bath
8'-8" Clg.

Dining Room
12'-0" x 14'-10"
9'-0" to 10'-0"
Stepped Clg.

Up

WIC

Master Bath
10'-0" Clg.

Make-up Area
Whirlpool

Garage
22'-2" x 31'-4"
7'-6" Clg.

Art Niche

Foyer
Open to Above

Built-Ins

Study
12'-0" x 16'-0"
13'-0" to 14'-0"
Beamed Clg.

Master Garden

Walk-In Shower

Entry
Barrel Vault

©THE SATER DESIGN COLLECTION, INC.

main level

Bedroom 2
11'-7" x 15'-3"
9'-4" Clg.

WIC

Guest Bath
9'-4" Clg.

Bath 2
9'-4" Clg.

Open to Below
21'-0" to 22'-2"
Coffered Clg.

Guest Suite
14'-0" x 13'-4"
9'-4" Clg.

WIC

Walk-In Shower

Walk-In Shower

Attic Space

Computer Desk

Loft
9'-8" Clg.

Dn

Balcony
9'-8" Clg.

Dn

WIC

Bedroom 1
11'-8" x 13'-2"
9'-0" Clg.

Open to Below
23'-0" to 24'-4"
Beamed Clg.

Art Niche

Dn

Walk-In Shower

Bath 1
8'-0" Clg.

Bonus Room
12'-0" x 21'-2"
5'-0" to 8'-0"
Vaulted Clg.

21'-0" x 22'-4"
Beamed Clg.

Plant Shelf

©THE SATER DESIGN COLLECTION, INC.

upper level

rear elevation

© The Sater Design Collection, Inc.

www.saterdesign.com

© The Sater Design Collection, Inc.

Coach Hill

HARMONY HOUSE — *Sleek forms and rural aesthetics mingle with this traditional yet hip design—a satisfying blend suited for neo-neighborhoods and chic burbs.*

Powerful arrangements of inner spaces that progress from an intimate entry to a wide-open casual zone propose a purposeful visual experience within this English country design. The foyer surrounds a high-glam staircase, enhanced with a dome ceiling and clerestory windows that bring in light. A stepped ceiling and arched columns define the forward formal dining room, permitting an unobstructed view of the rear property from the front of the home. Plenty of natural light enters the interior through the two-story bow window in the great room, which shares a two-sided fireplace with the adjoining study. French doors open this space and the master suite to a private veranda—a great place for moon-gazing and quiet conversation. The owners' retreat brags a bay window, an ample dressing area, and access to an outdoor garden from the master bath.

PLAN | *8013*

Bedroom: 4   Width: 70'0"

Bath: 4-1/2   Depth: 100'0"

Foundation: Slab or
   optional basement

Exterior Walls: 2x6

Main Level: 3,018 sq ft

Upper Level: 1,646 sq ft

Living Area: 4,664 sq ft

Bonus Room: 294 sq ft

Price Code: **L2**

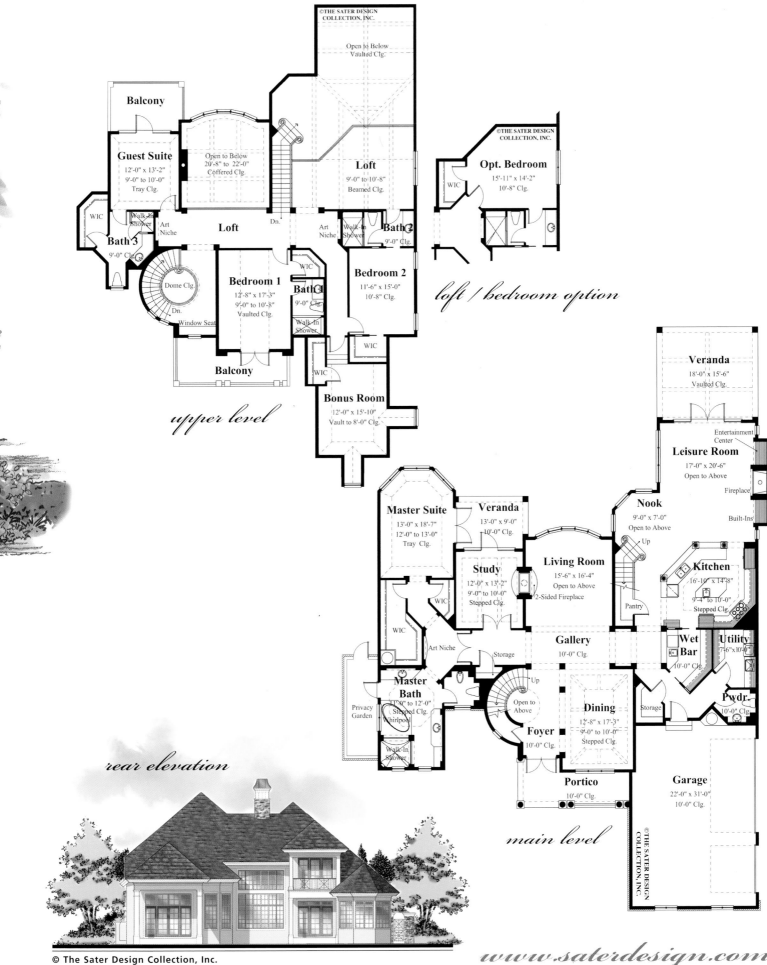

©THE SATER DESIGN COLLECTION, INC.

Open to Below
Vaulted Clg.

Balcony

Guest Suite
12'-0" x 13'-2"
9'-0" to 10'-0"
Tray Clg.

Open to Below
20'-8" to 22'-0"
Coffered Clg.

Loft
9'-0" to 10'-8"
Beamed Clg.

©THE SATER DESIGN
COLLECTION, INC.

Opt. Bedroom
15'-11" x 14'-2"
10'-8" Clg.

WIC

WIC

Walk-In
Shower

Art Niche

Loft

Dn.

Art
Niche

Walk-In
Shower

Bath 2
9'-0" Clg.

loft / bedroom option

Bath 3
9'-0" Clg.

Dome Clg.

Dn.

Bedroom 1
12'-8" x 17'-3"
9'-0" to 10'-8"
Vaulted Clg.

WIC

Bath 1
9'-0" Clg.

Walk-In
Shower

Bedroom 2
11'-6" x 15'-0"
10'-8" Clg.

WIC

Window Seat

WIC

Balcony

WIC

Bonus Room
12'-0" x 15'-10"
Vault to 8'-0" Clg.

upper level

Veranda
18'-0" x 15'-6"
Vaulted Clg.

Entertainment
Center

Leisure Room
17'-0" x 20'-6"
Open to Above

Fireplace

Built-Ins

Master Suite
13'-0" x 18'-7"
12'-0" to 13'-0"
Tray Clg.

Veranda
13'-0" x 9'-0"
10'-0" Clg.

Nook
9'-0" x 7'-0"
Open to Above

Up

Kitchen
16'-10" x 14'-8"

9'-4" to 10'-0"
Stepped Clg.

Study
12'-0" x 13'-2"
9'-0" to 10'-0"
Stepped Clg.

Living Room
15'-6" x 16'-4"
Open to Above
2-Sided Fireplace

Pantry

WIC

WIC

Art Niche

Storage

Gallery
10'-0" Clg.

**Wet
Bar**

Utility
7'-6" x 10'-0"
10'-0" Clg.

**Master
Bath**
11'-9" to 12'-0"
Stepped Clg.
Whirlpool

Up

Open to
Above

Storage

Pwdr.
10'-0" Clg.

Privacy
Garden

Walk-In
Shower

Foyer
10'-0" Clg.

Dining
12'-8" x 17'-3"
9'-0" to 10'-0"
Stepped Clg.

rear elevation

Portico
10'-0" Clg.

Garage
22'-0" x 31'-0"
10'-0" Clg.

main level

©THE SATER DESIGN
COLLECTION, INC.

www.saterdesign.com

© The Sater Design Collection, Inc.

Aubrey

SIMPLY PARADISE — *Banana-hued stucco and leaf shutters wrap familiar lines with a contemporary disposition—bold and new—to go with a sweet personality.*

Wrought-iron balustrades, shed rooflines and sculpted masonry define a classic elevation that is anchored by a stunning side turret, twin dormers and massive Doric columns. The romantic theme creates a stunning street presence, in step with neo-neighborhood relationships. The design ethos continues into the forward rooms, which introduce a fabulous layout—dramatic, inspiring and deeply comfortable. Grand arches and columns frame the foyer and gallery, flanked by well-defined formal rooms. At the heart of the home, a spacious leisure room leads to the lanai, and brags a through-fireplace shared with a private study. The opposing turret harbors a winding staircase and a loft that links with a balcony hall and sleeping quarters. One of the secondary suites provides access to a rambling deck, near the bonus room, which resides above the rear-loading garage.

PLAN	*8016*

Bedroom: 4	Width: 83'0"
Bath: 3-1/2	Depth: 71'8"

Foundation: Slab
  or optional basement
Exterior Walls: 2x6

Main Level:	2,484 sq ft
Upper Level:	1,127 sq ft

Living Area:	3,611 sq ft
Bonus Room:	332 sq ft

Price Code: **L1**

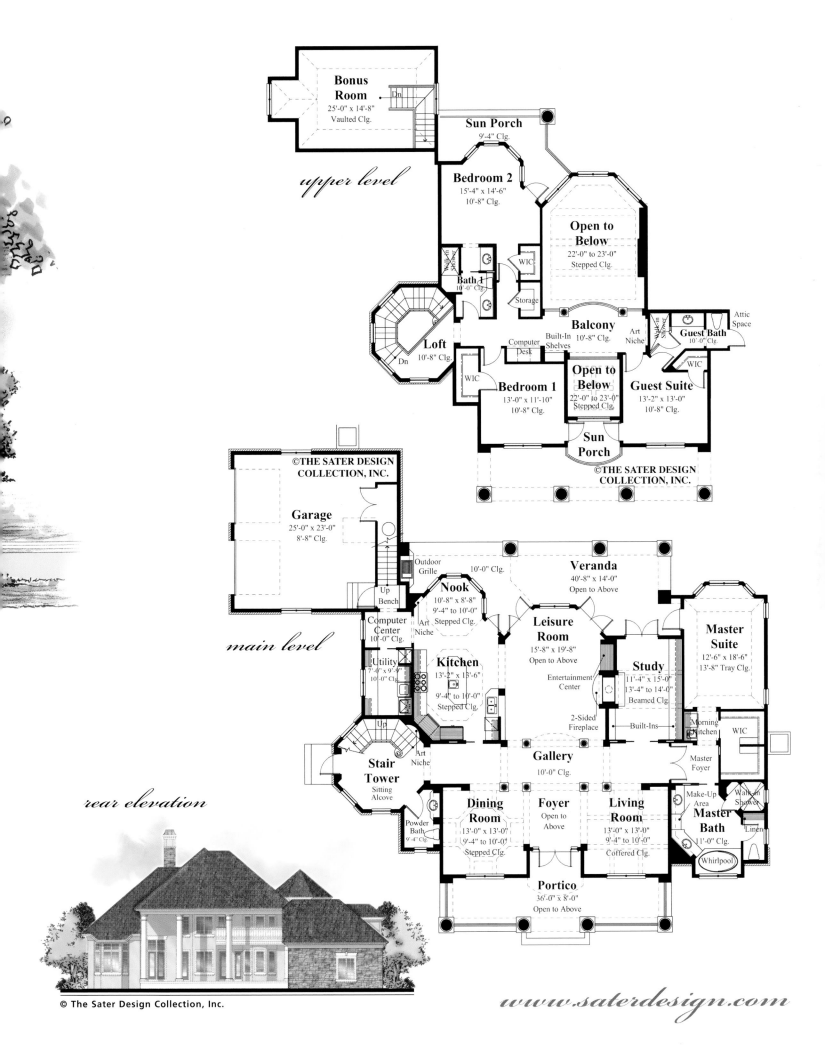

upper level

Bonus Room
25'-0" x 14'-8"
Vaulted Clg.

Dn

Sun Porch
9'-4" Clg.

Bedroom 2
15'-4" x 14'-6"
10'-8" Clg.

Open to Below
22'-0" to 23'-0"
Stepped Clg.

WIC

Bath 1
10'-0" Clg.

Storage

Balcony
10'-8" Clg.

Built-In Shelves

Art Niche

Walk-In Shower

Guest Bath
10'-0" Clg.

Attic Space

Loft
10'-8" Clg.

Dn

Computer Desk

WIC

Bedroom 1
13'-0" x 11'-10"
10'-8" Clg.

Open to Below
22'-0" to 23'-0"
Stepped Clg.

Guest Suite
13'-2" x 13'-0"
10'-8" Clg.

WIC

Sun Porch

Garage
25'-0" x 23'-0"
8'-8" Clg.

main level

Up Bench

Outdoor Grille

10'-0" Clg.

Nook
10'-8" x 8'-8"
9'-4" to 10'-0"
Stepped Clg.

Veranda
40'-8" x 14'-0"
Open to Above

Computer Center
10'-0" Clg.

Art Niche

Leisure Room
15'-8" x 19'-8"
Open to Above

Master Suite
12'-6" x 18'-6"
13'-8" Tray Clg.

Utility
7'-0" x 9'-9"
10'-0" Clg.

Kitchen
13'-2" x 13'-6"
9'-4" to 10'-0"
Stepped Clg.

Entertainment Center

Study
11'-4" x 15'-0"
13'-4" to 14'-0"
Beamed Clg.

Up

Built-Ins

Morning Kitchen

WIC

Stair Tower
Sitting Alcove

Art Niche

2-Sided Fireplace

Master Foyer

rear elevation

Powder Bath
9'-4" Clg.

Gallery
10'-0" Clg.

Make-Up Area

Walk-In Shower

Dining Room
13'-0" x 13'-0"
9'-4" to 10'-0"
Stepped Clg.

Foyer
Open to Above

Living Room
13'-0" x 13'-0"
9'-4" to 10'-0"
Coffered Clg.

Master Bath
11'-0" Clg.

Linen

Whirlpool

Portico
36'-0" x 8'-0"
Open to Above

www.saterdesign.com

© The Sater Design Collection, Inc.

Ascott

GLOBAL GLAMOUR — *Sunshine and vanilla tones warm this contemporary villa with timeless seaside serenity—and speak softly of the English countryside.*

Great vintage lines recall strokes of genius from 19th-century British architecture and blissfully marry history with a contemporary sanctuary. Prevailing summer breezes will find their way from the enchanting double portico, through many joyful rooms, to the rear veranda. French doors and bay windows invite fresh air and panoramic views to reside in private and public realms—which can flex to suit the changing lifestyles of the owners. A friends' entry and side staircase leads to secondary and guest quarters, which could accommodate a live-in relative or teenager, or grow into a game room for the entire family. A gallery loft on this level sports a built-in desk and shelves, overlooking a spectacular great room and leading to a sun porch.

PLAN | 8019

Bedroom: 4   Width: 80'0"

Bath: 4-1/2   Depth: 63'8"

Foundation: Slab or
    optional basement

Exterior Walls: 2x6

Main Level: 2,227 sq ft

Upper Level: 1,278 sq ft

Living Area: 3,505 sq ft

Price Code: **L1**

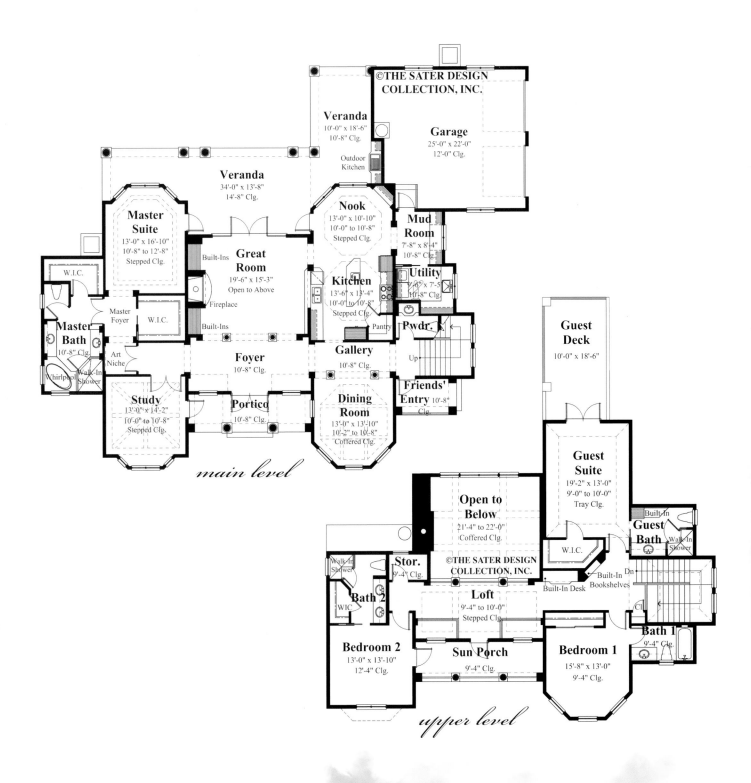

Garage
25'-0" x 22'-0"
12'-0" Clg.

Veranda
10'-0" x 18'-6"
10'-8" Clg.

Outdoor Kitchen

Veranda
34'-0" x 13'-8"
14'-8" Clg.

Nook
13'-0" x 10'-10"
10'-0" to 10'-8"
Stepped Clg.

Mud Room
7'-8" x 8'-4"
10'-8" Clg.

Master Suite
13'-0" x 16'-10"
10'-8" to 12'-8"
Stepped Clg.

W.I.C.

Built-Ins

Great Room
19'-6" x 15'-3"
Open to Above

W.I.C.

Kitchen
13'-6" x 13'-4"
10'-0" to 10'-8"
Stepped Clg.

Utility
9'-6" x 7'-5"
10'-8" Clg.

Master Bath
10'-8" Clg.

Master Foyer

Fireplace

Built-Ins

Pantry

Pwdr.

Whirlpool

Walk-In Shower

Art Niche

Gallery
10'-8" Clg.

Up

Foyer
10'-8" Clg.

Friends' Entry 10'-8" Clg.

Study
13'-0" x 14'-2"
10'-0" to 10'-8"
Stepped Clg.

Portico
10'-8" Clg.

Dining Room
13'-0" x 13'-10"
10'-2" to 10'-8"
Coffered Clg.

main level

Guest Deck
10'-0" x 18'-6"

Guest Suite
19'-2" x 13'-0"
9'-0" to 10'-0"
Tray Clg.

Built-In

Guest Bath

Walk-In Shower

Open to Below
21'-4" to 22'-0"
Coffered Clg.

W.I.C.

Walk-In Shower

Stor.
9'-4" Clg.

Built-In Desk

Built-In Bookshelves

Dn

Bath 2

WIC

Loft
9'-4" to 10'-0"
Stepped Clg.

Clg.

Bath 1
9'-4" Clg.

Bedroom 2
13'-0" x 13'-10"
12'-4" Clg.

Sun Porch
9'-4" Clg.

Bedroom 1
15'-8" x 13'-0"
9'-4" Clg.

upper level

rear elevation

Edmonton

RUSTIC AND REFINED — *Rough stone and rafter tails recall the elemental architecture of 16th-century rural England—rich with intractable rhythms of the country.*

A classic symmetry prevails throughout this plan, from the synchronized entry portico to the rear courtyard. Sculpted arcades and rambling terraces glide into airy, contemporary spaces that are designed for 21st-century living. A massive fireplace anchors the core of the plan —an open, linear arrangement of the foyer and great room—which is extended by the outdoor terrace. Gentle breezes and wide views infiltrate the casual zone from a loggia that boasts an outdoor kitchen and leads to the fountain, courtyard pool and spa. The master wing includes a secluded study and a powder bath—a convenient setup for temporary guest quarters. An interior door maintains privacy for the master suite, which begins with a sculpted art niche, or dressing mirror, and extends to a bay window overlooking the courtyard and fountain. A spiral staircase in the garage leads up a bow window to a splendid space that could be developed to hold a live-in relative or media room for the family's use.

PLAN | *8023*

Bedroom: 3 Width: 60'6"
Bath: 2-1/2 Depth: 94'0"
Foundation: Slab or optional basement
Exterior Walls: 2x6

Main Level: 2,117 sq ft
Upper Level: 652 sq ft

Living Area: 2,769 sq ft
Bonus Room: 375 sq ft

Price Code: **C3**

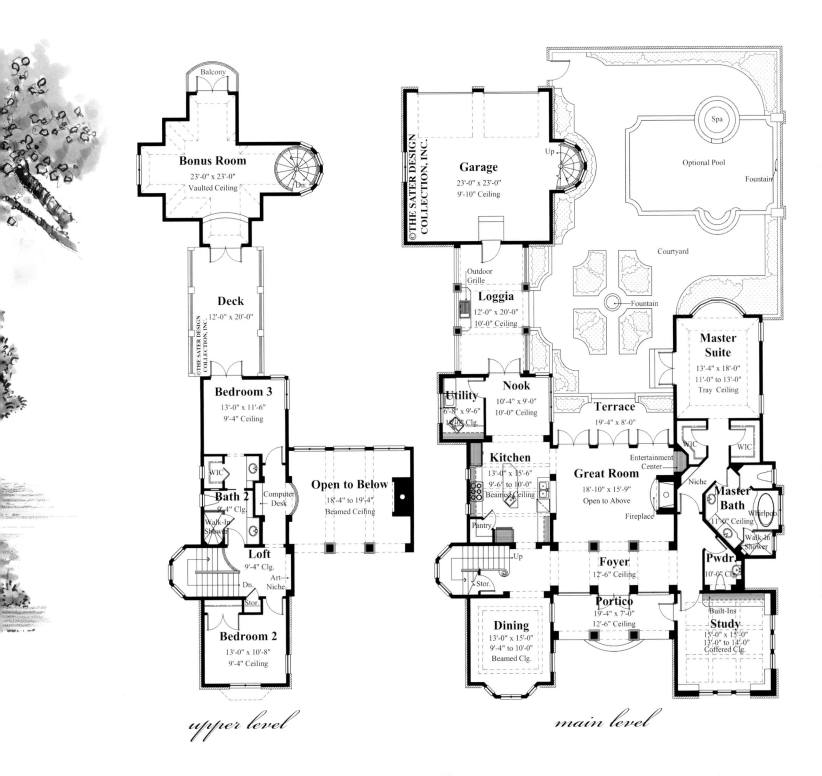

Bonus Room
23'-0" x 23'-0"
Vaulted Ceiling

Balcony

Dn.

Deck
12'-0" x 20'-0"

Bedroom 3
13'-0" x 11'-6"
9'-4" Ceiling

WIC

Bath 2
9'-4" Clg.

Walk-In Shower

Computer Desk

Open to Below
18'-4" to 19'-4"
Beamed Ceiling

Loft
9'-4" Clg.

Dn.

Art Niche

Stor.

Bedroom 2
13'-0" x 10'-8"
9'-4" Ceiling

upper level

© THE SATER DESIGN COLLECTION, INC.

Garage
23'-0" x 23'-0"
9'-10" Ceiling

Up

Spa

Optional Pool

Fountain

Courtyard

Fountain

Outdoor Grille

Loggia
12'-0" x 20'-0"
10'-0" Ceiling

Nook
10'-4" x 9'-0"
10'-0" Ceiling

Utility
6'-8" x 9'-6"
14'-10" Clg.

Terrace
19'-4" x 8'-0"

Master Suite
13'-4" x 18'-0"
11'-0" to 13'-0"
Tray Ceiling

WIC

WIC

Kitchen
13'-0" x 15'-6"
9'-6" to 10'-0"
Beamed Ceiling

Great Room
18'-10" x 15'-9"
Open to Above

Entertainment Center

Niche

Master Bath
11'-0" Ceiling

Whirlpool

Fireplace

Pantry

Walk-In Shower

Foyer
12'-6" Ceiling

Up

Pwdr.
10'-0" Clg.

Portico
19'-4" x 7'-0"
12'-6" Ceiling

Stor.

Dining
13'-0" x 15'-0"
9'-4" to 10'-0"
Beamed Clg.

Built-Ins

Study
15'-0" x 15'-0"
13'-0" to 14'-0"
Coffered Clg.

main level

rear elevation

www.saterdesign.com

© The Sater Design Collection, Inc.

© The Sater Design Collection, Inc.

Bellamare

DREAM WEAVER — *Derived from a classic British vocabulary, colonial and tropical details establish an Old World provenance brimming with coastal panache.*

An appealing blend of stone and stucco defines this quintessential European facade and conveys the charm of the British countryside. Graceful arches, fanlights and wrought-iron balustrades complement a towering bay and a massive stone arch framing the entry. Double doors lead to a grand foyer that serves as a spectacular stair hall, decked with classic columns and grand views. The central living space presents a formal composition designed for planned events and dining, enhanced with a two-sided fireplace shared with the library/study. To facilitate less formal meals, the main living areas open to a wraparound veranda that sports an outdoor grille. Upstairs, the gallery loft connects the primary sleeping quarters with a guest suite, and opens to a sun porch, which boasts a barrel ceiling.

PLAN | 8027

Bedroom: 5   Width: 58'0"

Bath: 5-1/2   Depth: 65'0"

Foundation: Slab or
  optional basement

Exterior Walls: 2x6

Main Level: 1,996 sq ft

Upper Level: 2,171 sq ft

Living Area: 4,167 sq ft

Price Code: **L2**

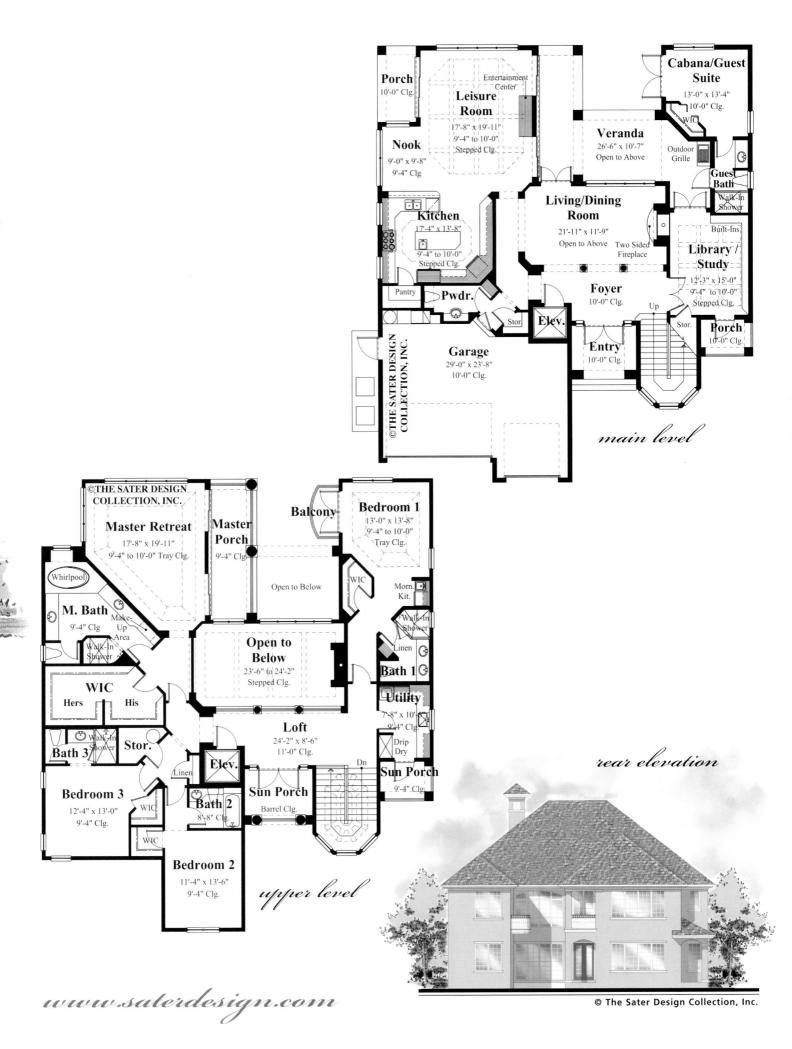

Porch
10'-0" Clg.

Leisure Room
17'-8" x 19'-11"
9'-4" to 10'-0"
Stepped Clg.

Entertainment Center

Cabana/Guest Suite
13'-0" x 13'-4"
10'-0" Clg.

WIC

Nook
9'-0" x 9'-8"
9'-4" Clg.

Veranda
26'-6" x 10'-7"
Open to Above

Outdoor Grille

Guest Bath
Walk-In Shower

Kitchen
17'-4" x 13'-8"
9'-4" to 10'-0"
Stepped Clg.

Living/Dining Room
21'-11" x 11'-9"
Open to Above

Two Sided Fireplace

Built-Ins

Library / Study
12'-3" x 15'-0"
9'-4" to 10'-0"
Stepped Clg.

Pantry

Pwdr.

Foyer
10'-0" Clg.

Up

Stor.

Elev.

Entry
10'-0" Clg.

Stor.

Porch
10'-0" Clg.

©THE SATER DESIGN COLLECTION, INC.

Garage
29'-0" x 23'-8"
10'-0" Clg.

main level

©THE SATER DESIGN COLLECTION, INC.

Master Retreat
17'-8" x 19'-11"
9'-4" to 10'-0" Tray Clg.

Master Porch
9'-4" Clg.

Balcony

Bedroom 1
13'-0" x 13'-8"
9'-4" to 10'-0"
Tray Clg.

Whirlpool

M. Bath
9'-4" Clg.

Make-Up Area

Open to Below

WIC

Walk-In Shower

Morn. Kit.

WIC
Hers   His

Walk-In Shower

Open to Below
23'-6" to 24'-2"
Stepped Clg.

Linen

Bath 1

Bath 3

Stor.

Utility
7'-8" x 10'-
9'-4" Clg.

Linen

Elev.

Bedroom 3
12'-4" x 13'-0"
9'-4" Clg.

WIC

Loft
24'-2" x 8'-6"
11'-0" Clg.

Drip Dry

Bath 2
8'-8" Clg.

Sun Porch
Barrel Clg.

Dn

Sun Porch
9'-4" Clg.

WIC

Bedroom 2
11'-4" x 13'-6"
9'-4" Clg.

upper level

rear elevation

www.saterdesign.com

© The Sater Design Collection, Inc.

English | REVIVAL

Hamilton

PERIOD PIECE — *Slump arches, double columns and a roofline balustrade nudge this historic Euro design to the cutting edge without losing its vintage cool.*

Freely interpreted revival elements empower a country theme with this neo-English manor—its true beauty, though, lies beyond its glass-paneled entry. A deeply comfortable interior, bright with windows and natural light, boasts new-century form and ground-level function. Formal rooms frame the foyer, a vaulted, well-lit space with a coffered ceiling. The great room boasts plenty of fresh air and views, with three sets of French doors leading out to the veranda. An extended-hearth fireplace and built-ins oppose a kitchen pass-through—which invites movie nights at home for a crowd or just the family. A food-preparation island in the gourmet kitchen permits the serving of planned events. Secondary sleeping quarters cluster near the casual zone, while a secluded master suite offers repose for the owners. A dressing area flanked by walk-in closets extends the garden bath.

PLAN | *8029*

Bedroom: 3   Width: 62'10"

Bath: 2-1/2   Depth: 73'6"

Foundation: Slab or
   optional basement

Exterior Walls: 2x6

Main Level: 2,194 sq ft

Living Area: 2,194 sq ft

Price Code: **C2**

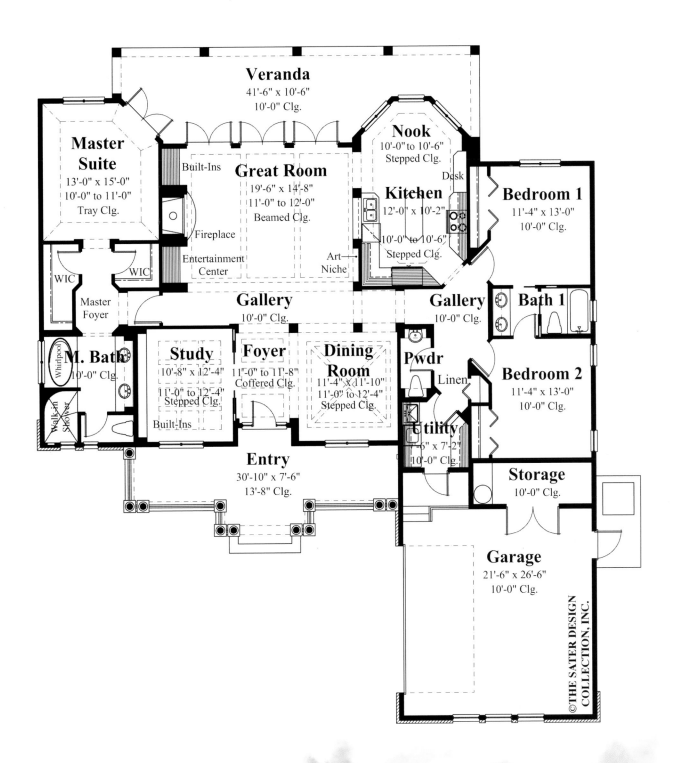

Veranda
41'-6" x 10'-6"
10'-0" Clg.

Master Suite
13'-0" x 15'-0"
10'-0" to 11'-0"
Tray Clg.

Built-Ins

Great Room
19'-6" x 14'-8"
11'-0" to 12'-0"
Beamed Clg.

Nook
10'-0" to 10'-6"
Stepped Clg.

Desk

Kitchen
12'-0" x 10'-2"
10'-0" to 10'-6"
Stepped Clg.

Bedroom 1
11'-4" x 13'-0"
10'-0" Clg.

Fireplace

Entertainment Center

Art Niche

WIC

WIC

Master Foyer

Gallery
10'-0" Clg.

Gallery
10'-0" Clg.

Bath 1

M. Bath
10'-0" Clg.

Study
10'-8" x 12'-4"
11'-0" to 12'-4"
Stepped Clg.

Built-Ins

Foyer
11'-0" to 11'-8"
Coffered Clg.

Dining Room
11'-4" x 11'-10"
11'-0" to 12'-4"
Stepped Clg.

Pwdr

Linen

Bedroom 2
11'-4" x 13'-0"
10'-0" Clg.

Whirlpool

Walk-in Shower

Utility
6" x 7'-2"
10'-0" Clg.

Entry
30'-10" x 7'-6"
13'-8" Clg.

Storage
10'-0" Clg.

Garage
21'-6" x 26'-6"
10'-0" Clg.

©THE SATER DESIGN COLLECTION, INC.

rear elevation

www.saterdesign.com

© The Sater Design Collection, Inc.

Gullane

PROPER MANOR — *Sunlit balconies and open-air loggias assign a New World twist to a traditional English vernacular—with a seaside panache that's merely comfortable.*

Rows of windows punctuate a smooth cocoa-hued stucco facade, which integrates historic Euro lines with an oceanfront attitude. The spirit throughout the house is formal yet inviting enough to extend a sense of welcome to guests, and provide satisfying repose for the owners. A paradise of open spaces framed by gently arched galleries, beamed ceilings and half-walls takes on the future with wired and culinary capabilities. Stainless steel appliances and an into-the-future entertainment center counter a massive fireplace, beamed ceilings and a walk-in wine cellar. The design ethos continues upstairs, where big and bold open spaces offer an airy joie d'vivre extension of traditional, well-defined rooms. Three secondary suites offer accommodations for guests, space for a nursery or sleeping quarters for family members. An entire wing is dedicated to the owners' retreat, which provides a private sun porch.

PLAN	*8031*

Bedroom: 5   Width: 58'0"

Bath: 5-1/2   Depth: 65'0"

Foundation: Slab or
   optional basement

Exterior Walls: 2x6

Main Level: 2,164 sq ft

Upper Level: 2,311 sq ft

Living Area: 4,475 sq ft

Price Code: **L2**

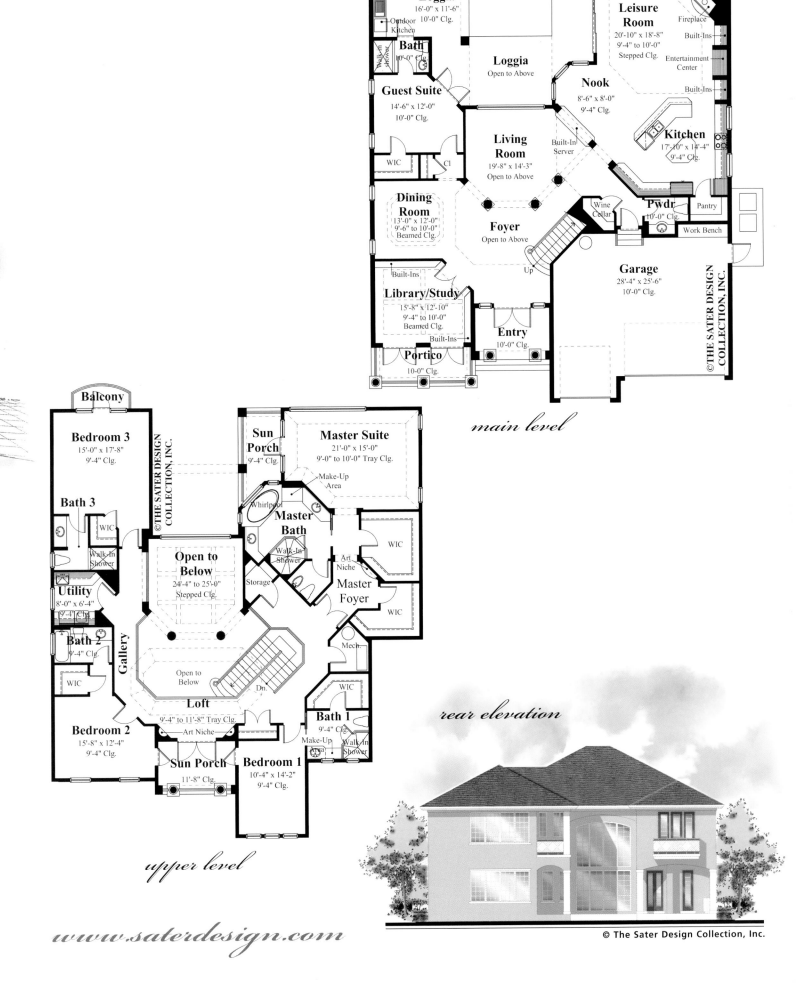

Loggia
16'-0" x 11'-6"
10'-0" Clg.

Outdoor Kitchen

Bath
10'-0"

Walk-In Shower

Leisure Room
20'-10" x 18'-8"
9'-4" to 10'-0"
Stepped Clg.

Fireplace

Built-Ins

Loggia
Open to Above

Nook
8'-6" x 8'-0"
9'-4" Clg.

Entertainment Center

Built-Ins

Guest Suite
14'-6" x 12'-0"
10'-0" Clg.

Living Room
19'-8" x 14'-3"
Open to Above

Kitchen
17'-10" x 14'-4"
9'-4" Clg.

WIC   Cl.

Built-In Server

Dining Room
13'-0" x 12'-0"
9'-6" to 10'-0"
Beamed Clg.

Foyer
Open to Above

Wine Cellar

Pwdr
10'-0" Clg.

Pantry

Work Bench

Built-Ins

Library/Study
15'-8" x 12'-10"
9'-4" to 10'-0"
Beamed Clg.

Up

Garage
28'-4" x 25'-6"
10'-0" Clg.

Entry
10'-0" Clg.

Built-Ins

Portico
10'-0" Clg.

©THE SATER DESIGN COLLECTION, INC.

main level

Balcony

Bedroom 3
15'-0" x 17'-8"
9'-4" Clg.

©THE SATER DESIGN COLLECTION, INC.

Sun Porch
9'-4" Clg.

Master Suite
21'-0" x 15'-0"
9'-0" to 10'-0" Tray Clg.

Make-Up Area

Bath 3

WIC

Walk-In Shower

Whirlpool

Master Bath

WIC

Open to Below
24'-4" to 25'-0"
Stepped Clg.

Walk-In Shower

Art Niche

Utility
8'-0" x 6'-4"
9'-4" Clg.

Storage

Master Foyer

Gallery

WIC

Bath 2
9'-4" Clg.

Mech.

WIC

Loft
9'-4" to 11'-8" Tray Clg.

Open to Below

Dn.

Art Niche

Bath 1
9'-4" Clg.

Bedroom 2
15'-8" x 12'-4"
9'-4" Clg.

Make-Up Area

Walk-In Shower

Sun Porch
11'-8" Clg.

Bedroom 1
10'-4" x 14'-2"
9'-4" Clg.

rear elevation

upper level

www.saterdesign.com

English | GOTHIC

© The Sater Design Collection, Inc.

Maitena

INNER SPACE — *Lancet windows with intersecting Gothic tracery, transoms and side panels establish a stunning presence, evocative of 18th-century England.*

Simple finials and gothic arches reinforce the style and set off the symmetrical forms of this European country facade. A smooth stucco arcade plays counterpoint to highly textured, rustic stone gables—expressing an ancient harmony that's precisely suited to today's vital neighborhoods. The breezy entry portico complements a wrapping rear lanai, with a cabana bath and an outdoor kitchen. Retreating walls open the leisure and living rooms to the outside amenities and invite a sense of nature into the casual zone. A walk-in wet bar adjoins the kitchen and provides a servery to the formal dining room. Stepped ceilings help to define the public realm, which leads to a pool-bath area of the lanai. To the right of the plan, the master wing employs two bay windows to bring in sunlight—or moonlight. Room-sized walk-in closets frame a dressing space that leads to a garden bath with separate vanities.

PLAN | *8036*

Bedroom: 3   Width: 83'10"
Bath: 4   Depth: 106'0"
Foundation: Slab
Exterior Walls: 2x6

Main Level: 3,942 sq ft

Living Area: 3,942 sq ft

Price Code: **L1**

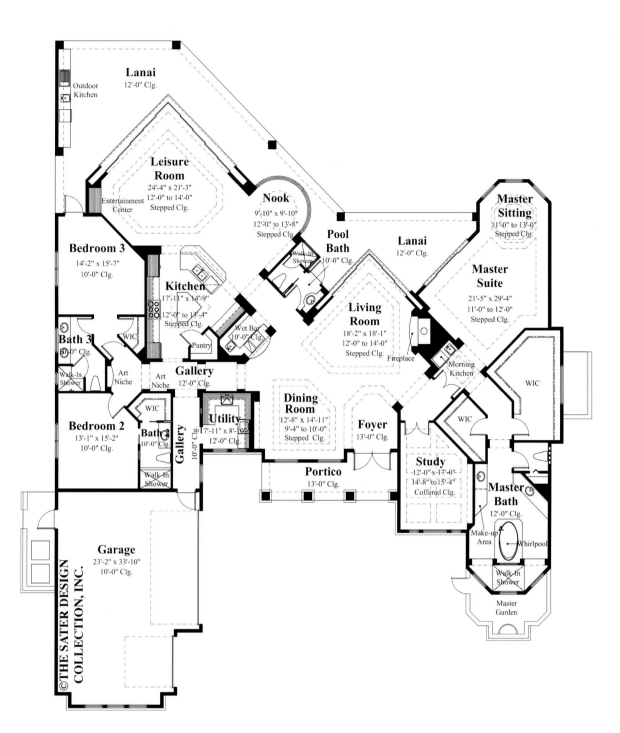

Lanai
12'-0" Clg.

Outdoor Kitchen

Leisure Room
24'-4" x 21'-3"
12'-0" to 14'-0"
Stepped Clg.

Nook
9'-10" x 9'-10"
12'-0" to 13'-8"
Stepped Clg.

Master Sitting
11'-0" to 13'-0"
Stepped Clg.

Pool Bath
10'-0" Clg.

Lanai
12'-0" Clg.

Entertainment Center

Walk-In Shower

Master Suite
21'-5" x 29'-4"
11'-0" to 12'-0"
Stepped Clg.

Bedroom 3
14'-2" x 15'-7"
10'-0" Clg.

Kitchen
17'-11" x 14'-9"
12'-0" to 13'-4"
Stepped Clg.

Living Room
18'-2" x 18'-1"
12'-0" to 14'-0"
Stepped Clg.

Bath 3
10'-0" Clg.

WIC

Wet Bar
10'-0" Clg.

Pantry

Fireplace

Morning Kitchen

WIC

Walk-In Shower

Art Niche

Art Niche

Gallery
12'-0" Clg.

WIC

Bedroom 2
13'-1" x 15'-2"
10'-0" Clg.

WIC

Bath 2
10'-0" Clg.

Gallery
10'-0" Clg.

Utility
7'-11" x 8'-0"
12'-0" Clg.

Dining Room
12'-8" x 14'-11"
9'-4" to 10'-0"
Stepped Clg.

Foyer
13'-0" Clg.

Study
12'-0" x 17'-0"
14'-8" to 15'-4"
Coffered Clg.

Master Bath
12'-0" Clg.

Walk-In Shower

Make-up Area

Whirlpool

Portico
13'-0" Clg.

Master Garden

Garage
23'-2" x 33'-10"
10'-0" Clg.

©THE SATER DESIGN COLLECTION, INC.

rear elevation

© The Sater Design Collection, Inc.

Chadwick — ELEVATION A

CHARM AND COMFORT — *Vintage lines honor the rural English provenance of this rustic manor—with an artful mix of past and present that prevails throughout the home.*

Quoins and stone lintels complement the sculpted entry of this manor elevation, enriched with stacked stone and terra-hued stucco. Inside, large windows and French doors are employed to bring in natural light and to visually extend the living spaces. Ceiling treatments—rustic and smooth—define the open, no-boundaries rooms of the central interior. A bumped-out bay window harbors a morning nook and brings in a sense of nature shared with the gourmet kitchen. The wrapping lanai invites parties and open air dining, with access from the great room, formal dining room and nook. Careful architecture provides privacy and defined areas for a forward study and for the master suite. Upstairs, a loft links two family bedrooms that share a sun deck.

PLAN	8038

Bedroom: 3   Width: 72'0"

Bath: 3-1/2   Depth: 68'3"

Foundation: Slab or
   optional basement

Exterior Walls: 2x6

Main Level: 2,250 sq ft
Upper Level: 663 sq ft

Living Area: 2,913 sq ft
Bonus Room: 351 sq ft

Price Code: **C3**

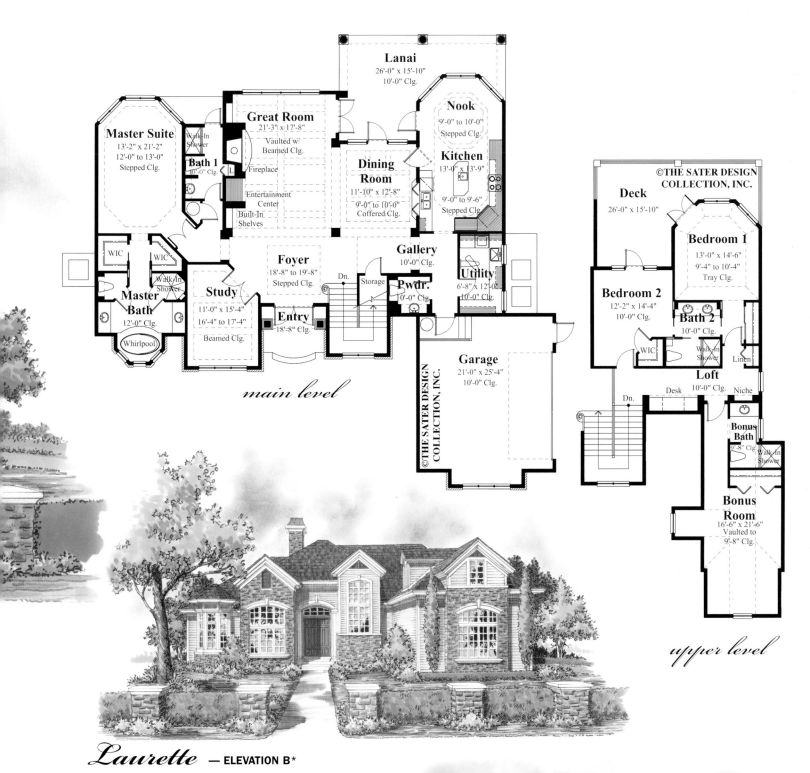

Master Suite
13'-2" x 21'-2"
12'-0" to 13'-0"
Stepped Clg.

Walk-In Shower

Bath 1
10'-0" Clg.

Great Room
21'-3" x 17'-8"
Vaulted w/ Beamed Clg.

Fireplace

Entertainment Center

Built-In Shelves

Lanai
26'-0" x 15'-10"
10'-0" Clg.

Nook
9'-0" to 10'-0"
Stepped Clg.

Kitchen
13'-0" x 13'-9"
9'-0" to 9'-6"
Stepped Clg.

Dining Room
11'-10" x 12'-8"
9'-0" to 10'-0"
Coffered Clg.

WIC

WIC

Walk-In Shower

Master Bath
12'-0" Clg.

Whirlpool

Study
11'-0" x 15'-4"
16'-4" to 17'-4"
Beamed Clg.

Foyer
18'-8" to 19'-8"
Stepped Clg.

Entry
18'-8" Clg.

Dn.

Storage

Gallery
10'-0" Clg.

Pwdr.
0'-0" Clg.

Utility
6'-8" x 12'-0"
10'-0" Clg.

Garage
21'-0" x 25'-4"
10'-0" Clg.

©THE SATER DESIGN COLLECTION, INC.

main level

Deck
26'-0" x 15'-10"

©THE SATER DESIGN COLLECTION, INC.

Bedroom 1
13'-0" x 14'-6"
9'-4" to 10'-4"
Tray Clg.

Bedroom 2
12'-2" x 14'-4"
10'-0" Clg.

Bath 2
10'-0" Clg.

WIC

Walk-In Shower

Linen

Loft
10'-0" Clg.

Desk

Dn.

Niche

Bonus Bath
9'-8" Clg.

Walk-In Shower

Bonus Room
16'-6" x 21'-6"
Vaulted to 9'-8" Clg.

upper level

Laurette — ELEVATION B*

* call for plan details

rear elevation

www.saterdesign.com

© The Sater Design Collection, Inc.

Wellington

RIVAL INSTINCTS — *Neoclassical lines shelter an array of arched windows and a truly inviting entry—capped by a trio of traditional dormers and framed by twin chimneys.*

Evocative of early revival homes, this European manor melds a highly sophisticated brick-and-stucco facade with the kind of livable amenities that endear a home to its owners. A gallery foyer defined by arches and columns grants vistas that extend from the entry to the rear veranda—via an airy living/dining room with a vaulted beamed ceiling. A series of French doors bordering the master and living wings eases a transition from inside to outside, leading to a rambling veranda that encompasses a grille and cabana bath. A food-prep counter in the well-planned kitchen overlooks a glass morning bay and a leisure room with retreating walls that access a private area of the veranda. With an original approach to the everyday, a side gallery connects two secondary bedrooms with a utility wing, mud room and, ultimately, the casual zone of the house.

PLAN	*8041*

Bedroom: 3   Width: 84'0"

Bath: 2 Full &   Depth: 92'0"
2 Half

Foundation: Slab

Exterior Walls: 2x6

Main Level: 3,351 sq ft

Living Area: 3,351 sq ft

Price Code: **C4**

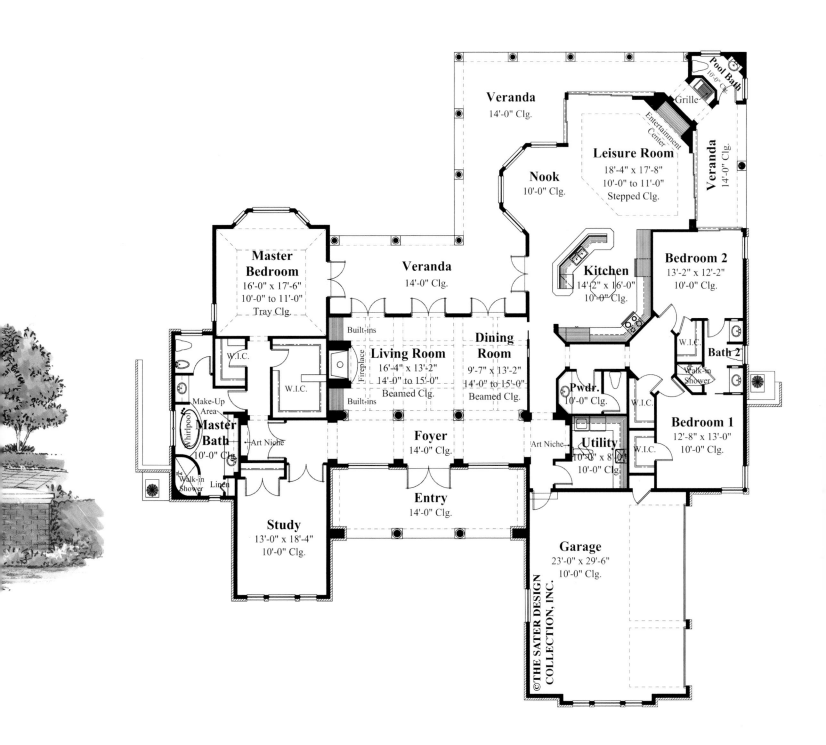

Veranda
14'-0" Clg.

Pool Bath
10'-0" Clg.

Grille

Entertainment Center

Leisure Room
18'-4" x 17'-8"
10'-0" to 11'-0"
Stepped Clg.

Veranda
14'-0" Clg.

Master Bedroom
16'-0" x 17'-6"
10'-0" to 11'-0"
Tray Clg.

Veranda
14'-0" Clg.

Nook
10'-0" Clg.

Kitchen
14'-2" x 16'-0"
10'-0" Clg.

Bedroom 2
13'-2" x 12'-2"
10'-0" Clg.

W.I.C.

W.I.C.

Bath 2

W.I.C.

Built-ins

Living Room
16'-4" x 13'-2"
14'-0" to 15'-0"
Beamed Clg.

Dining Room
9'-7" x 13'-2"
14'-0" to 15'-0"
Beamed Clg.

Fireplace

Built-ins

Pwdr.
10'-0" Clg.

Walk-in Shower

Make-Up Area

Whirlpool

Master Bath
10'-0" Clg.

Art Niche

Foyer
14'-0" Clg.

Art Niche

Utility
10'-0" x 8'
10'-0" Clg.

W.I.C.

Bedroom 1
12'-8" x 13'-0"
10'-0" Clg.

Walk-in Shower

Linen

Entry
14'-0" Clg.

Study
13'-0" x 18'-4"
10'-0" Clg.

Garage
23'-0" x 29'-6"
10'-0" Clg.

©THE SATER DESIGN COLLECTION, INC.

rear elevation

© The Sater Design Collection, Inc.

Demetri

BEAU VILLA — *Sun-filled rooms, wide-open views and the perfect mix of relaxed and formal create a new brand of history house—with a look that tugs at the heart.*

Stately Corinthian columns and a trio of pediments set off this revival facade. An ornamented medallion plays harmony with circular transom windows and a fanlight above the glass-paneled entry. Two chimneys confirm the classic symmetry of the elevation, which employs a hipped roofline, pilasters and forward gables to balance its presentation. The interior progresses from the foyer and formal rooms to a grand central living space that flexes to facilitate planned events as well as cozy family gatherings. As the plan unfolds to the right, halls lead separately to the airy, indoor/outdoor casual zone and to the secondary bedrooms. Secluded to the other side of the home, a distinctive master suite provides plenty of space and luxurious amenities for two owners. An alternative plan offers an optional bedroom in place of the game room.

PLAN | *8045*

Bedroom: 4   Width: 80'0"

Bath: 3-1/2   Depth: 108'0"

Foundation: Slab or
    optional basement

Exterior Walls: 2x6

Main Level: 3,764 sq ft

Living Area: 3,764 sq ft

Price Code: **L1**

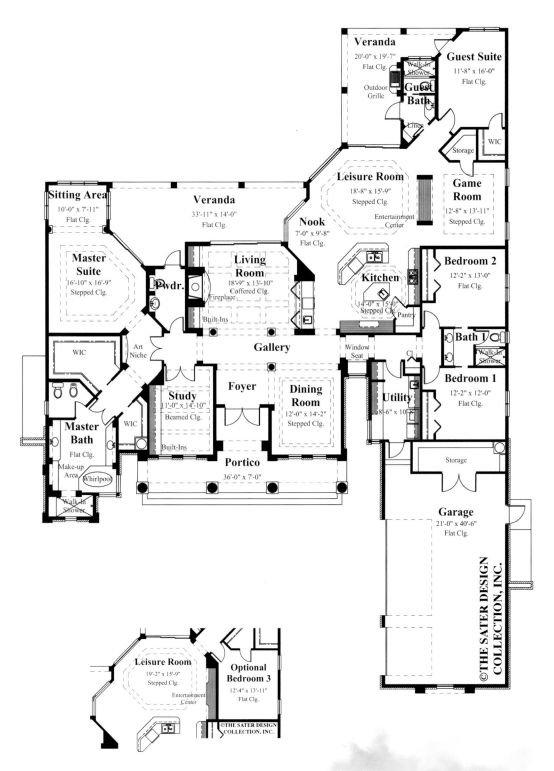

Veranda
20'-0" x 19'-7"
Flat Clg.

Outdoor
Grille

Guest
Bath

Walk-In
Shower

Guest Suite
11'-8" x 16'-0"
Flat Clg.

Linen

WIC

Storage

Sitting Area
10'-0" x 7'-11"
Flat Clg.

Veranda
33'-11" x 14'-0"
Flat Clg.

Leisure Room
18'-8" x 15'-9"
Stepped Clg.

Entertainment
Center

Game Room
12'-8" x 13'-11"
Stepped Clg.

Master Suite
16'-10" x 16'-9"
Stepped Clg.

Nook
7'-0" x 9'-8"
Flat Clg.

Living Room
18'-9" x 13'-10"
Coffered Clg.

Fireplace

Built-Ins

Pwdr.

Kitchen
14'-0" x 15'-0"
Stepped Clg.

Pantry

Bedroom 2
12'-2" x 13'-0"
Flat Clg.

WIC

Art
Niche

Gallery

Window
Seat

Cl

Bath 1

Walk-In
Shower

Master Bath
Flat Clg.

WIC

Study
11'-0" x 14'-10"
Beamed Clg.

Built-Ins

Foyer

Dining Room
12'-0" x 14'-2"
Stepped Clg.

Utility
8'-6" x 10'

Bedroom 1
12'-2" x 12'-0"
Flat Clg.

Make-up
Area

Whirlpool

Walk-In
Shower

Portico
36'-0" x 7'-0"

Storage

Garage
21'-0" x 40'-6"
Flat Clg.

©THE SATER DESIGN COLLECTION, INC.

Leisure Room
19'-2" x 15'-9"
Stepped Clg.

Entertainment
Center

Optional Bedroom 3
12'-4" x 13'-11"
Flat Clg.

©THE SATER DESIGN COLLECTION, INC.

rear elevation

© The Sater Design Collection, Inc.

Garnett

HISTORY HOUSE — *Pedimented, pale-linen gables reinforce the pure, symmetrical geometry of this classic British revival facade, which harbors a courtyard.*

Cultured stone accents twist a classic vocabulary of pilasters, columns and perfectly-scaled proportions toward a comfortable, 21st-century look. Varied rooflines and staggered gables command a powerful street presence yet conceal an enchanting courtyard. Beyond a breezy portico and secluded guest suite, the courtyard leads to the formal entry via a loggia, which provides a corner fireplace and shelter from the sun. A paneled door opens to the foyer and an open interior with bay windows that extend the footprint of the home. To the left of the public realm, a splendid owners' retreat with private access to the rear loggia provides built-in cabinetry and a garden bath with separate lavs and walk-in closets. The foyer stairs ascend to an upper gallery that links three secondary bedrooms and two full baths.

PLAN | *8047*

Bedroom: 5   Width: 80'0"
Bath: 4-1/2   Depth: 96'6"
Foundation: Slab
Exterior Walls: 2x6

Main Level: 2,852 sq ft
Upper Level: 969 sq ft
Guest Suite: 330 sq ft

Living Area: 4,151 sq ft

Price Code: **L2**

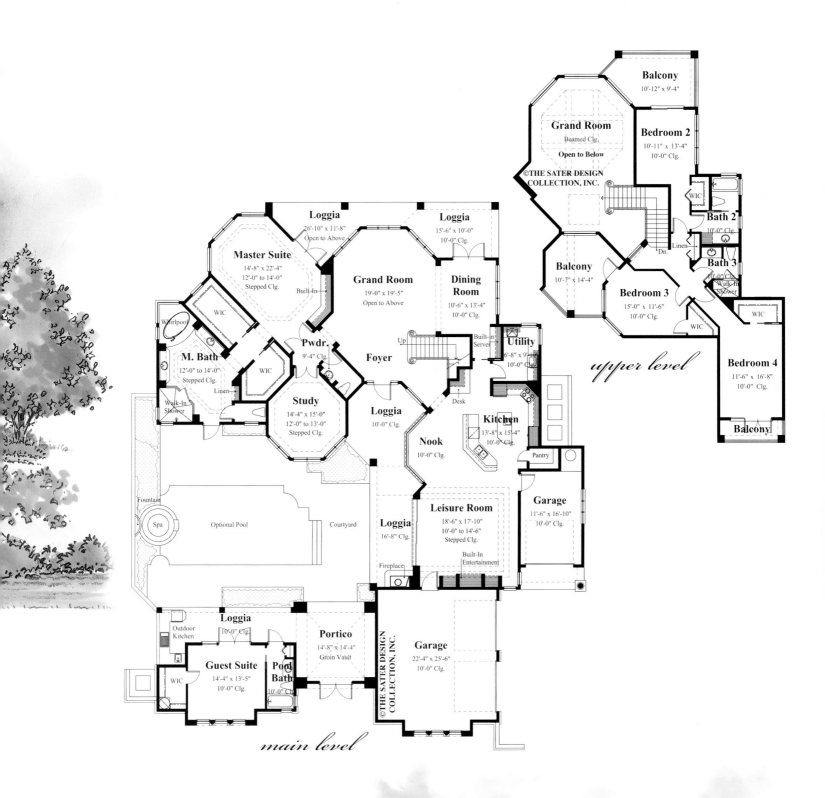

Balcony
10'-12" x 9'-4"

Grand Room
Beamed Clg.

Open to Below

©THE SATER DESIGN
COLLECTION, INC.

Bedroom 2
10'-11" x 13'-4"
10'-0" Clg.

WIC

Bath 2
10'-0" Clg.

Bath 3
10'-0" Clg.
Walk-In
Shower

Linen

Balcony
10'-7" x 14'-4"

Bedroom 3
15'-0" x 11'-6"
10'-0" Clg.

WIC

WIC

upper level

Bedroom 4
11'-6" x 16'-8"
10'-0" Clg.

Balcony

Loggia
26'-10" x 11'-8"
Open to Above

Loggia
15'-6" x 10'-0"
10'-0" Clg.

Master Suite
14'-8" x 22'-4"
12'-0" to 14'-0"
Stepped Clg.

WIC

Built-In

Grand Room
19'-0" x 19'-5"
Open to Above

Dining Room
10'-6" x 13'-4"
10'-0" Clg.

Whirlpool

M. Bath
12'-0" to 14'-0"
Stepped Clg.

WIC

Pwdr.
9'-4" Clg.

Foyer

Up

Built-In
Server

Utility
6'-8" x 9'-1"
10'-0" Clg.

Walk-In
Shower

Linen

Study
14'-4" x 15'-0"
12'-0" to 13'-0"
Stepped Clg.

Loggia
10'-0" Clg.

Desk

Nook
10'-0" Clg.

Kitchen
13'-8" x 15'-4"
10'-0" Clg.

Pantry

Fountain

Spa

Optional Pool

Courtyard

Loggia
16'-8" Clg.

Leisure Room
18'-6" x 17'-10"
10'-0" to 14'-6"
Stepped Clg.

Garage
11'-6" x 16'-10"
10'-0" Clg.

Fireplace

Built-In
Entertainment

Outdoor
Kitchen

Loggia
10'-0" Clg.

Guest Suite
14'-4" x 13'-5"
10'-0" Clg.

WIC

Pool Bath
10'-0" Clg.

Portico
14'-8" x 14'-4"
Groin Vault

©THE SATER DESIGN
COLLECTION, INC.

Garage
22'-4" x 25'-6"
10'-0" Clg.

main level

rear elevation

www.saterdesign.com

© The Sater Design Collection, Inc.

English | COTSWOLD

© The Sater Design Collection, Inc.

Huxford

COTSWOLD COMES HOME — *Earth-hued stone turrets pronounce elements of the familiar Cotswold vernacular—yet this timeless architecture goes a little wild.*

Powerful forms address the streetscape with this English Country home. A recessed entry opens to an unexpected outdoor space that proceeds through a magnificent courtyard to the formal entry. Near the outer portal, a guest house offers a cabana-style bath and opens to an eating area of the courtyard, complete with a grille and food-prep area. Near the front door, a separate sitting area designed for conversation provides a fireplace. Inside the home, the foyer melds with the grand room and links two private zones: the master suite and the casual living space. In the leisure room, a built-in entertainment center anchors an area that encompasses the morning nook and kitchen. A pocket door protects guests from kitchen noises in the formal dining room—which, through French doors, opens to a private loggia.

PLAN | *8048*

Bedroom: 5   Width: 80'0"
Bath: 4-1/2   Depth: 96'0"
Foundation: Slab
Exterior Walls: 2x6

Main Level: 2,852 sq ft
Upper Level: 969 sq ft
Guest Suite: 337 sq ft

Living Area: 4,158 sq ft

Price Code: **L2**

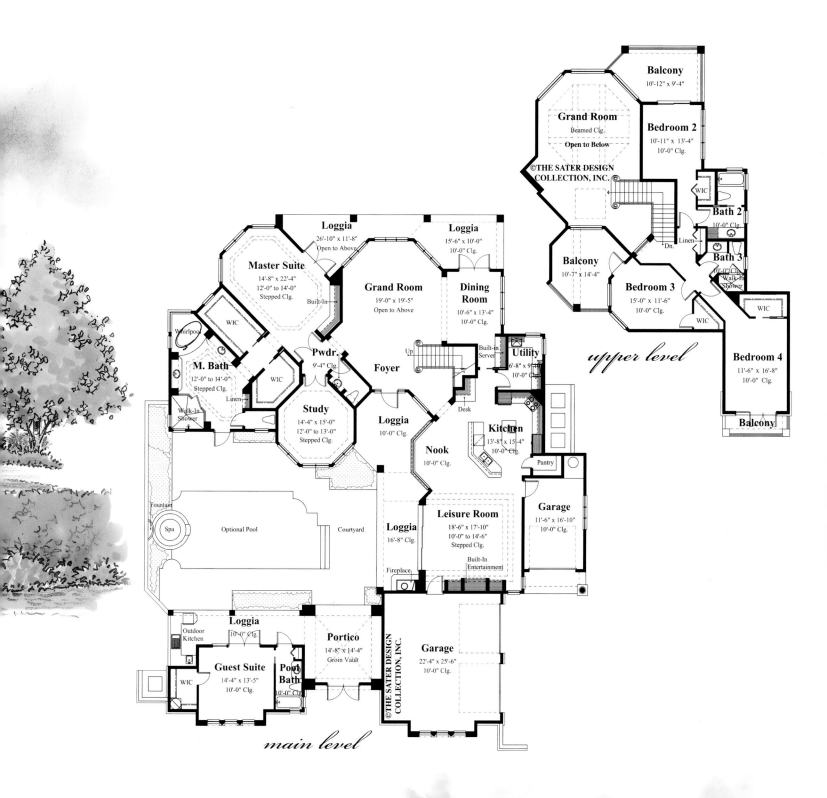

Balcony
10'-12" x 9'-4"

Grand Room
Beamed Clg.
Open to Below

©THE SATER DESIGN
COLLECTION, INC.

Bedroom 2
10'-11" x 13'-4"
10'-0" Clg.

WIC

Bath 2
10'-0" Clg.

Linen

Bath 3
10'-0" Clg.

Walk-In Shower

Balcony
10'-7" x 14'-4"

Dn.

Bedroom 3
15'-0" x 11'-6"
10'-0" Clg.

WIC

WIC

Bedroom 4
11'-6" x 16'-8"
10'-0" Clg.

Balcony

upper level

Loggia
26'-10" x 11'-8"
Open to Above

Loggia
15'-6" x 10'-0"
10'-0" Clg.

Master Suite
14'-8" x 22'-4"
12'-0" to 14'-0"
Stepped Clg.

Built-In

Grand Room
19'-0" x 19'-5"
Open to Above

Dining Room
10'-6" x 13'-4"
10'-0" Clg.

Whirlpool

WIC

Pwdr.
9'-4" Clg.

Foyer

Up

Built-In Server

Utility
6'-8" x 9'-4"
10'-0" Clg.

M. Bath
12'-0" x 14'-0"
Stepped Clg.

WIC

Linen

Study
14'-4" x 15'-0"
12'-0" to 13'-0"
Stepped Clg.

Loggia
10'-0" Clg.

Desk

Walk-In Shower

Nook
10'-0" Clg.

Kitchen
13'-8" x 15'-4"
10'-0" Clg.

Pantry

Fountain

Spa

Optional Pool

Courtyard

Loggia
16'-8" Clg.

Leisure Room
18'-6" x 17'-10"
10'-0" to 14'-6"
Stepped Clg.

Garage
11'-6" x 16'-10"
10'-0" Clg.

Fireplace

Built-In Entertainment

Outdoor Kitchen

Loggia
10'-0" Clg.

Portico
14'-8" x 14'-4"
Groin Vault

Guest Suite
14'-4" x 13'-5"
10'-0" Clg.

Pool Bath
10'-0" Clg.

WIC

©THE SATER DESIGN COLLECTION, INC.

Garage
22'-4" x 25'-6"
10'-0" Clg.

main level

rear elevation

© The Sater Design Collection, Inc.

Kendrick

URBAN SPIRIT — *Clean lines reminiscent of our most revered city dwellings take on the soul of a country house, there to offer respite from a busy life.*

Gently carved balusters, square transoms and pure symmetry define this Neoclassic exterior, yet the design offers much more than a beautiful facade. A triplet of paneled doors leads through an open foyer to a spectacular great room with unimpeded views of the rear property. Art niches and a massive hearth define one wall of the great room, and contradict an opposing series of flat soffits that open the space to the kitchen. Zoned for servicing crowd-sized events or just snacks, the kitchen features a central island with a veggie sink, double ovens, a six-burner cooktop, a walk-in pantry and glamorous see-through cabinets. To the right of the plan, the master wing sports a splendid bath with a spa-style tub and a walk-in shower. Upstairs, a balcony loft links four family bedrooms and leads to the front balcony.

PLAN | *8050*

Bedroom: 5   Width: 72'0"
Bath: 3-1/2   Depth: 71'0"
Foundation: Slab
Exterior Walls: 2x6

Main Level: 2,163 sq ft
Upper Level: 1,415 sq ft
_____
Living Area: 3,578 sq ft

Price Code: **L1**

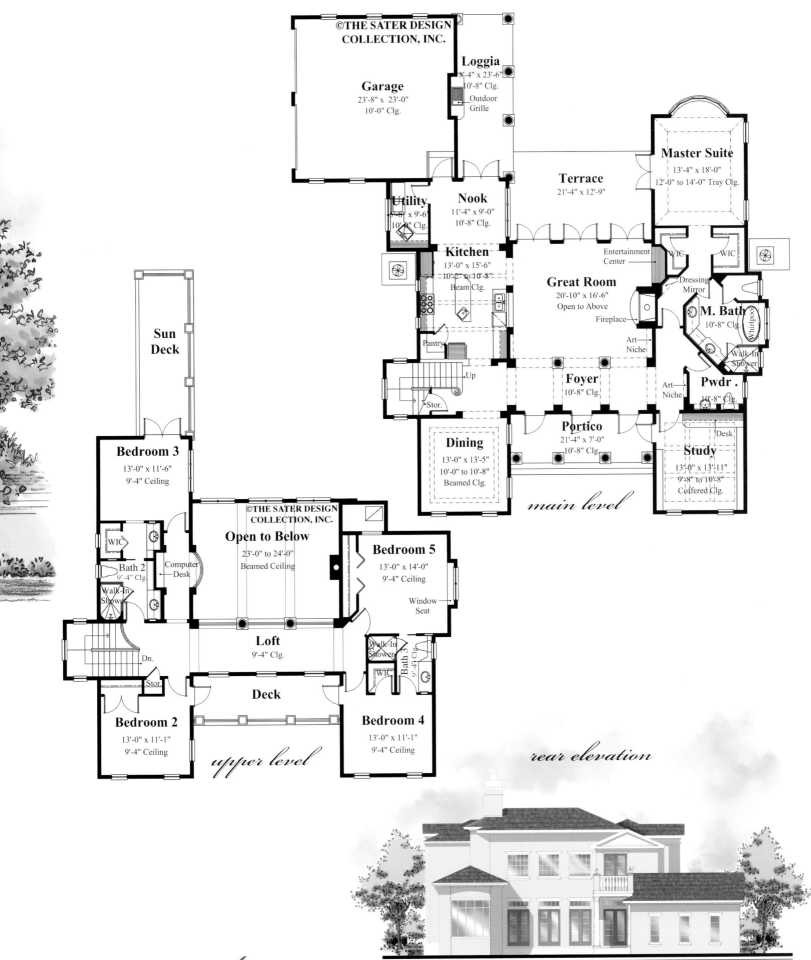

©THE SATER DESIGN COLLECTION, INC.

Garage
23'-8" x 23'-0"
10'-0" Clg.

Loggia
8'-4" x 23'-6"
10'-8" Clg.
Outdoor Grille

Terrace
21'-4" x 12'-9"

Master Suite
13'-4" x 18'-0"
12'-0" to 14'-0" Tray Clg.

Utility
x 9'-6"
10'-8" Clg.

Nook
11'-4" x 9'-0"
10'-8" Clg.

Kitchen
13'-0" x 15'-6"
10'-0" to 10'-8"
Beam Clg.

WIC

WIC

Great Room
20'-10" x 16'-6"
Open to Above

Entertainment Center

Dressing Mirror

M. Bath
10'-8" Clg.

Whirlpool

Pantry

Fireplace

Art Niche

Walk-In Shower

Sun Deck

Foyer
10'-8" Clg.

Up

Stor.

Art Niche

Pwdr.
10'-8" Clg.

Dining
13'-0" x 13'-5"
10'-0" to 10'-8"
Beamed Clg.

Portico
21'-4" x 7'-0"
10'-8" Clg.

Desk

Study
13'-0" x 13'-11"
9'-8" to 10'-8"
Coffered Clg.

main level

Bedroom 3
13'-0" x 11'-6"
9'-4" Ceiling

WIC

Bath 2
9'-4" Clg.

Computer Desk

Walk-In Shower

©THE SATER DESIGN COLLECTION, INC.

Open to Below
23'-0" to 24'-0"
Beamed Ceiling

Bedroom 5
13'-0" x 14'-0"
9'-4" Ceiling

Window Seat

Walk-In Shower

Bath 3
9'-4" Clg.

WIC

Dn.

Loft
9'-4" Clg.

Stor.

Deck

Bedroom 2
13'-0" x 11'-1"
9'-4" Ceiling

Bedroom 4
13'-0" x 11'-1"
9'-4" Ceiling

upper level

rear elevation

www.saterdesign.com

© The Sater Design Collection, Inc.

English | MANOR-STYLE

© The Sater Design Collection, Inc.

Ainsley

OUTER SPACE — *Imagine a place where the rhythm of days is commanded by the sun, and where temperature alone declares whether you are indoors or out.*

Matchstick trim and louvered shades call up houses of the coastal regions with this English country plan. A paneled door leads through the gallery and foyer to a rear courtyard, reinforcing an intimate link between nature and home. Open to the central hall, the formal rooms share the adventurous spirit of the heart of the home. A colonnade provides definition to the unrestrained spaces, and connects the master suite with clustered family bedrooms and with the casual living zone. The leisure room boasts a coffered ceiling and a well-crafted entertainment center. Steps from the dining room, the servery area of the kitchen includes a wet bar, and a walk-in pantry. The gourmet kitchen provides two island counters, double ovens and a six-burner cooktop. Outside, the lanai is equipped with an outdoor grille, while a side courtyard offers a fireplace.

PLAN	*8054*

Bedroom: 4	Width: 74'8"
Bath: 3-1/2	Depth: 118'0"
Foundation: Slab	
Exterior Walls: 2x6	
Main Level: 2,974 sq ft	
Guest Suite: 297 sq ft	
Living Area: 3,271 sq ft	
Price Code: **C4**	

Guest Suite
13'-0" x 16'-2"
10'-0" Clg.

Lanai
28'-8" x 27'-0"
10'-8" Clg.

Walk-In Shower

Outdoor Grille

Guest Bath
10'-0" Clg.

Master Suite
13'-4" x 20'-8"
10'-0" to 11'-0"
Stepped Clg.

Leisure Room
20'-6" x 18'-6"
10'-8" to 11'-8"
Coffered Clg.

Entertainment Center

WIC

WIC

Lanai
17'-0" x 12'-11"
10'-8" Clg.

Nook
10'-0" x 11'-5"
10'-8" Clg.

Lanai
11'-3" x 46'-0"
10'-8" Clg.

Art Niche

Kitchen
18'-0" x 15'-3"
10'-8" Clg.

Fireplace

Art Niche

Wet Bar

M. Bath
10'-0" Clg.

Whirlpool

Living Room
11'-6" x 14'-4"
12'-4" to 13'-4"
Coffered Clg.

Foyer
13'-4" Clg.

Dining
11'-8" x 14'-4"
12'-4" to 13'-4"
Stepped Clg.

Pantry

WIC

Bedroom 2
12'-0" x 12'-6"
10'-0" Clg.

Linen

Walk-In Shower

Pwdr.
10'-0" Clg.

Bath 2
10'-0" Clg.

Entry
13'-4" Clg.

Utility
8'-6" x 8'-0"
10'-0" Clg.

WIC

Bedroom 3
13'-6" x 14'-10"
10'-0" Clg.

Garage
23'-0" x 30'-10"
11'-4" Clg.

rear elevation

www.saterdesign.com

REGION/STYLE | *Spanish*

Mediterranean, Spanish Colonial and Revival—

here are homes deeply rooted in centuries-old Hispanic dialects,

drawn from many Mediterranean areas.

Sleek, simple lines surround fresh interpretations of courtyard styles.

Cantilevers and pavilions, decks and porticos

and cozy sheltered spaces create pleasing mixes of sunlight

and rooms that promise untamed views.

Spanish | ROMANESQUE

© The Sater Design Collection, Inc.

La Reina

CASA NUEVA — *An elaborate entry turret sets off this highly sculpted Spanish eclectic facade, yet hardly steals the show.*

Derived from a blend of cultural influences—including Moorish and Renaissance—this clearly Mediterranean elevation creates an impressive yet not imposing street presence. Trios of windows bring light to interior spaces, and accentuate rows of decorative tile vents that line the facade. Carved balusters enhance a side balcony that's spacious enough to serve as an outdoor room. The paneled portal opens to a portico and courtyard, which creates a procession to the formal entry of the home. To the front of the courtyard, a casita, or guest house, offers space that easily converts to a workshop or home office. The foyer opens directly to the grand room and, through an arched opening, to the formal dining room. Glass bayed walls in the central living area and in the study help meld inside and outside spaces, and the dining room leads to a loggia—for open air meals.

PLAN | *8046*

Bedroom: 5   Width: 80'0"
Bath: 4-1/2   Depth: 96'0"
Foundation: Slab
Exterior Walls: 2x6

Main Level: 2,852 sq ft
Upper Level: 969 sq ft
Guest Suite: 330 sq ft
_____
Living Area: 4,151 sq ft

Price Code: **L2**

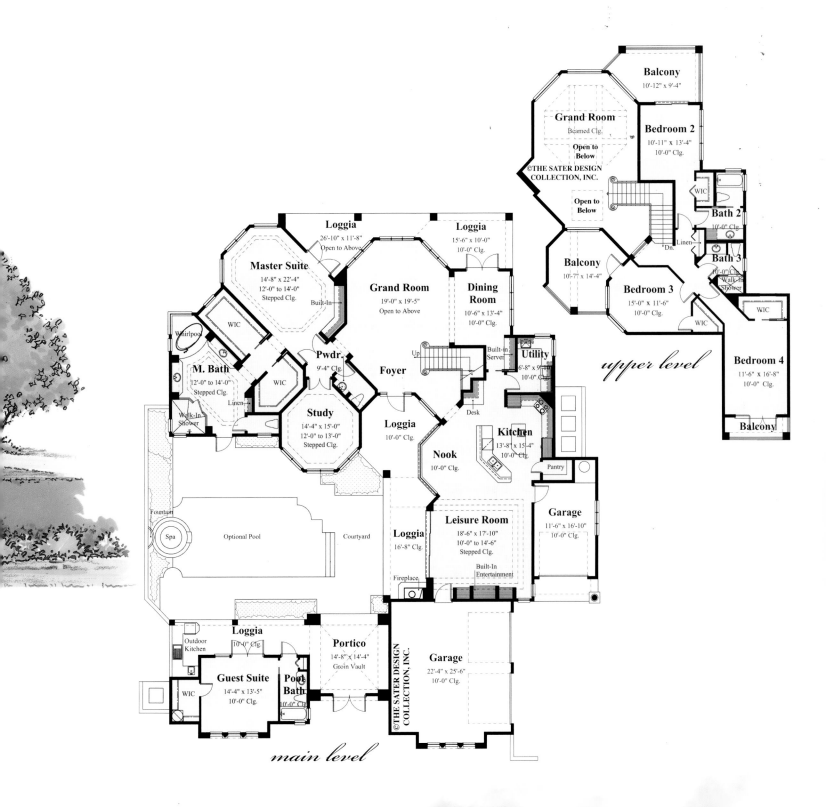

Balcony
10'-12" x 9'-4"

Grand Room
Beamed Clg.

Open to Below

©THE SATER DESIGN
COLLECTION, INC.

Open to Below

Bedroom 2
10'-11" x 13'-4"
10'-0" Clg.

WIC

Bath 2
10'-0" Clg.

Bath 3
10'-0" Clg.
Walk-In
Shower

Balcony
10'-7" x 14'-4"

Bedroom 3
15'-0" x 11'-6"
10'-0" Clg.

WIC

WIC

Bedroom 4
11'-6" x 16'-8"
10'-0" Clg.

Balcony

Linen

Dn.

upper level

Loggia
26'-10" x 11'-8"
Open to Above

Loggia
15'-6" x 10'-0"
10'-0" Clg.

Master Suite
14'-8" x 22'-4"
12'-0" to 14'-0"
Stepped Clg.

WIC

Built-In

Grand Room
19'-0" x 19'-5"
Open to Above

Dining Room
10'-6" x 13'-4"
10'-0" Clg.

Whirlpool

M. Bath
12'-0" to 14'-0"
Stepped Clg.

WIC

Pwdr.
9'-4" Clg.

Foyer

Up

Built-In
Server

Utility
6'-8" x 9'-11"
10'-0" Clg.

Linen

Walk-In
Shower

Study
14'-4" x 15'-0"
12'-0" to 13'-0"
Stepped Clg.

Loggia
10'-0" Clg.

Desk

Kitchen
13'-8" x 15'-4"
10'-0" Clg.

Pantry

Fountain

Spa

Optional Pool

Courtyard

Loggia
16'-8" Clg.

Nook
10'-0" Clg.

Leisure Room
18'-6" x 17'-10"
10'-0" to 14'-6"
Stepped Clg.

Garage
11'-6" x 16'-10"
10'-0" Clg.

Fireplace

Built-In
Entertainment

Loggia
10'-0" Clg.

Outdoor
Kitchen

Guest Suite
14'-4" x 13'-5"
10'-0" Clg.

WIC

Pool Bath
10'-0" Clg.

Portico
14'-8" x 14'-4"
Groin Vault

©THE SATER DESIGN
COLLECTION, INC.

Garage
22'-4" x 25'-6"
10'-0" Clg.

main level

rear elevation

www.saterdesign.com

© The Sater Design Collection, Inc.

© The Sater Design Collection, Inc.

Caprina

HACIENDA DEL MAR — *French doors and disappearing walls invite the sounds of the sea—and glimpses of moonlight—into a home designed for views of the horizon.*

Evocative of the adobe escapes of the Spanish Colonial vernacular, this exquisite villa invites a reconnection to nature and to a simple human need to slow down. A few powerful renaissance details, such as spiral pilasters and patterned masonry, twist the traditional vocabulary to a more modern, eclectic motif. Rows of arched-top windows enhance the sidewalk presence of the home, and bring plenty of light to the interior. Paneled doors lead to a grand foyer, which defies convention with a no-walls approach to the formal rooms. Coffered ceilings provide spatial separation and a visual link between the private and public realms. Dramatic views further define the interior and enable a rambling casual zone to meld into the scenery. A wraparound lanai connects public and private realms with an invitation to enjoy the outdoors, and perhaps meals alfresco.

PLAN | *8052*

Bedroom: 4	Width: 74'8"
Bath: 3-1/2	Depth: 118'0"
Foundation: Slab	
Exterior Walls: 2x6	

Main Level:	2,974 sq ft
Guest Suite:	297 sq ft

Living Area:	3,271 sq ft

Price Code: **C4**

Guest Suite
13'-0" x 16'-2"
10'-0" Clg.

Lanai
28'-8" x 27'-0"
10'-8" Clg.

Walk-In Shower

Guest Bath
10'-0" Clg.

Outdoor Grille

Master Suite
13'-4" x 20'-8"
10'-0" to 11'-0"
Stepped Clg.

Leisure Room
20'-6" x 18'-6"
10'-8" to 11'-8"
Coffered Clg.

Entertainment Center

Lanai
17'-0" x 12'-11"
10'-8" Clg.

Nook
10'-0" x 11'-5"
10'-8" Clg.

Lanai
11'-3" x 46'-0"
10'-8" Clg.

Fireplace

WIC

WIC

Kitchen
18'-0" x 15'-3"
10'-8" Clg.

Art Niche

Art Niche

Wet Bar

M. Bath
10'-0" Clg.

Pantry

Living Room
11'-6" x 14'-4"
12'-4" to 13'-4"
Coffered Clg.

Foyer
13'-4" Clg.

Dining
11'-8" x 14'-4"
12'-4" to 13'-4"
Stepped Clg.

Pwdr.
10'-0" Clg.

WIC

Bedroom 2
12'-0" x 12'-6"
10'-0" Clg.

Whirlpool

Linen

Walk-In Shower

Bath 2
10'-0" Clg.

Entry
13'-4" Clg.

Utility
8'-6" x 8'-0"
10'-0" Clg.

WIC

Bedroom 3
13'-6" x 14'-10"
10'-0" Clg.

Garage
23'-0" x 32'-10"
11'-4" Clg.

©THE SATER DESIGN COLLECTION, INC.

rear elevation

www.saterdesign.com

Spanish | ROMANESQUE

San Filippo

GREAT ADAPTATION — *Masonry details and rounded arches confirm the Spanish provenance of this design, while stately turrets suggest a Romanesque influence.*

Circular windows echo the curves of the arched transoms and sculpted colonnade of this striking facade. A deeply recessed entry plays counterpoint to two bold turrets that step into the landscape, extending the footprint of the home. Spacious, light-filled rooms allow unencumbered views throughout the interior. The pure geometry of the plan plays raw nature against historic details and 21st-century accoutrements. A massive hearth in the living room reinforces the ancient charm of tapered columns along the gallery, while French doors bring in scenery and light. Angled lines melt into the outdoors with walls of retreating glass in the morning nook and kitchen. Guests may step into a side courtyard from a flex room that easily converts to a study. A family valet, conveniently located, provides the perfect place to drop your keys and packages.

PLAN | *8055*

Bedroom: 5   Width: 69'4"
Bath: 4-1/2   Depth: 95'4"
Foundation: Slab or
    optional basement
Exterior Walls: 2x6 or 8" CBS

Main Level: 2,913 sq ft
Upper Level: 1,478 sq ft

Living Area: 4,391 sq ft

Price Code: **L2**

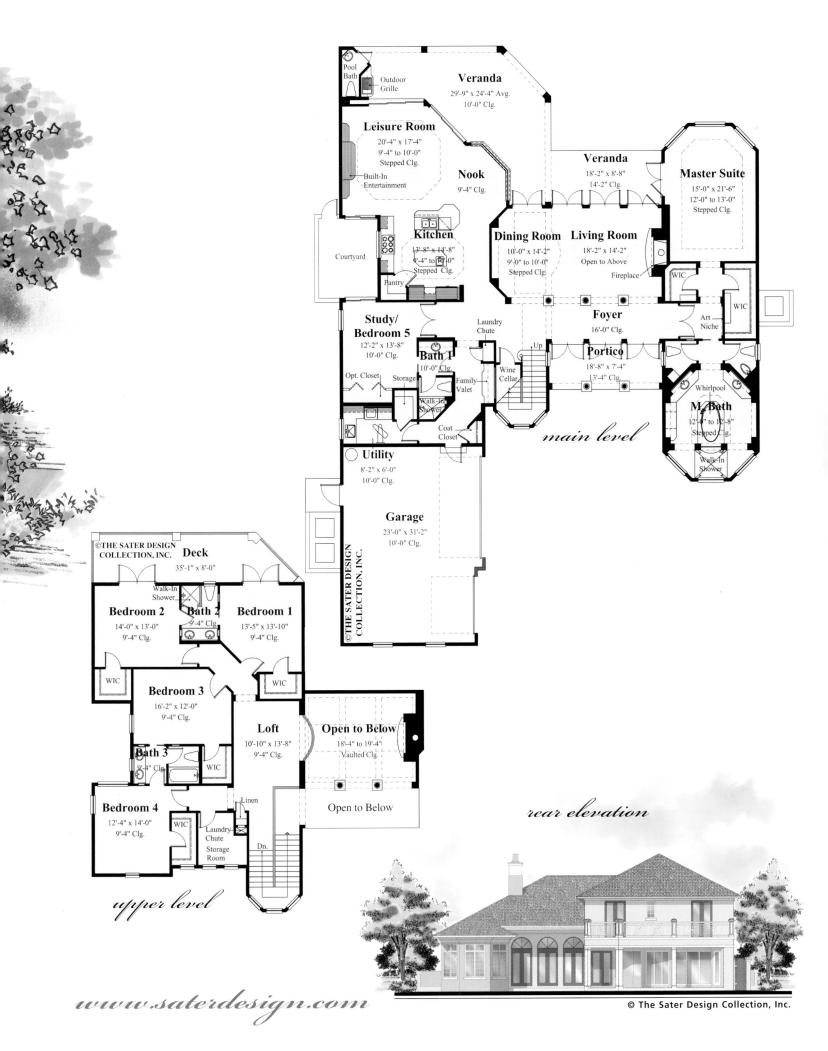

Pool Bath

Outdoor Grille

Veranda
29'-9" x 24'-4" Avg.
10'-0" Clg.

Leisure Room
20'-4" x 17'-4"
9'-4" to 10'-0"
Stepped Clg.

Built-In Entertainment

Nook
9'-4" Clg.

Veranda
18'-2" x 8'-8"
14'-2" Clg.

Master Suite
15'-0" x 21'-6"
12'-0" to 13'-0"
Stepped Clg.

Courtyard

Kitchen
13'-8" x 14'-8"
9'-4" to 10'-0"
Stepped Clg.

Pantry

Dining Room
10'-0" x 14'-2"
9'-0" to 10'-0"
Stepped Clg.

Living Room
18'-2" x 14'-2"
Open to Above

Fireplace

WIC

WIC

Foyer
16'-0" Clg.

Art Niche

Study/ Bedroom 5
12'-2" x 13'-8"
10'-0" Clg.

Laundry Chute

Bath 1
10'-0" Clg.

Opt. Closet

Storage

Family Valet

Wine Cellar

Up

Portico
18'-8" x 7'-4"
13'-4" Clg.

Whirlpool

M. Bath
12'-0" to 12'-8"
Stepped Clg.

Walk-In Shower

Walk-In Shower

Coat Closet

main level

Utility
8'-2" x 6'-0"
10'-0" Clg.

Garage
23'-0" x 31'-2"
10'-0" Clg.

Deck
35'-1" x 8'-0"

Walk-In Shower

Bedroom 2
14'-0" x 13'-0"
9'-4" Clg.

Bath 2
9'-4" Clg.

Bedroom 1
13'-5" x 13'-10"
9'-4" Clg.

WIC

WIC

Bedroom 3
16'-2" x 12'-0"
9'-4" Clg.

Loft
10'-10" x 13'-8"
9'-4" Clg.

Open to Below
18'-4" to 19'-4"
Vaulted Clg.

Bath 3
9'-4" Clg.

WIC

Bedroom 4
12'-4" x 14'-0"
9'-4" Clg.

WIC

Linen

Open to Below

Laundry Chute Storage Room

Dn.

upper level

rear elevation

© The Sater Design Collection, Inc.

Porta Rossa

GREAT ESCAPE — *An elaborate entry turret provides an absolutely perfect highlight to this hip, history-rich retreat.*

Decorative tile reveals, spiral pilasters and wrought-iron window treatments achieve a seamless fusion with the powerful, new-century look of this modern revival elevation. Low-pitched rooflines stay true to this home's Spanish heritage. A carved entry extends an inviting welcome. Interior vistas mix it up with sunlight and fresh breezes through the plan, with walls of glass that extend living spaces to the outdoors. A high-beamed ceiling, crafted cabinetry and a massive hearth achieve a colonial character that is seamlessly fused with tomorrow-land style: retreating walls, wide-open rooms, and sleek, do-everything appliances. The high-glam master suite boasts a step-up, spa-style tub, a garden wall and a futuristic frameless, walk-in shower. Two secondary bedrooms cluster around a shared bath with compartmented lavs, while the guest suite offers a cabana-style bath with access from the lanai. A family valet, conveniently located, provides the perfect place to drop your keys and packages.

PLAN | *8058*

Bedroom: 4   Width: 67'0"
Bath: 3-1/2   Depth: 91'8"
Foundation: Slab
Exterior Walls: 8"CBS or 2x6

Main Level: 3,105 sq ft

Living Area: 3,105 sq ft

Price Code: **C4**

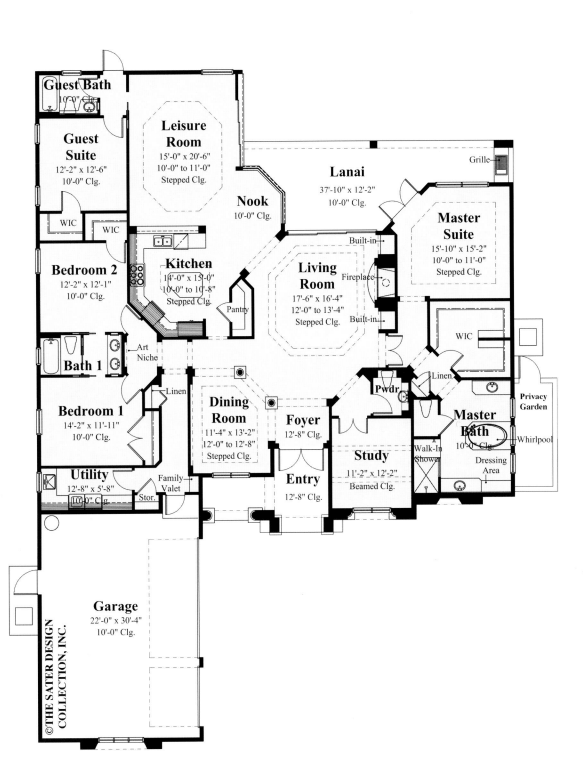

Guest Bath
10'-0" Clg.

Guest Suite
12'-2" x 12'-6"
10'-0" Clg.

Leisure Room
15'-0" x 20'-6"
10'-0" to 11'-0"
Stepped Clg.

Lanai
37'-10" x 12'-2"
10'-0" Clg.

Grille

Nook
10'-0" Clg.

Master Suite
15'-10" x 15'-2"
10'-0" to 11'-0"
Stepped Clg.

WIC   WIC

Bedroom 2
12'-2" x 12'-1"
10'-0" Clg.

Kitchen
14'-0" x 15'-0"
10'-0" to 10'-8"
Stepped Clg.

Living Room
17'-6" x 16'-4"
12'-0" to 13'-4"
Stepped Clg.

Fireplace

Built-in

Built-in

WIC

Pantry

Bath 1

Art Niche

Linen

Master Bath
10'-0" Clg.

Pwdr

Privacy Garden

Bedroom 1
14'-2" x 11'-11"
10'-0" Clg.

Linen

Dining Room
11'-4" x 13'-2"
12'-0" to 12'-8"
Stepped Clg.

Foyer
12'-8" Clg.

Walk-In Shower

Whirlpool

Dressing Area

Utility
12'-8" x 5'-8"
10'-0" Clg.

Family Valet

Stor.

Entry

Study
11'-2" x 12'-2"
Beamed Clg.
12'-8" Clg.

Garage
22'-0" x 30'-4"
10'-0" Clg.

© THE SATER DESIGN COLLECTION, INC.

rear elevation

© The Sater Design Collection, Inc.

Martelli

CASA GRANDE — *An eye-catching turret highlights this Spanish eclectic elevation, which sets off the streetscape and calls up the past.*

Hearty corbels cap a crafted pediment enhanced with a wrought-iron balcony on this high-glam coastal design. A sculpted, recessed entry defines the finely detailed facade, and a quatrefoil window confirms a Moorish influence. Inside, an open arrangement of the foyer and the formal rooms permits natural light to flow freely through the space. Walls of glass to the rear of the plan open the public and private realms of the interior to spectacular views. The casual living space includes a morning nook that overlooks the lanai. With double ovens, a six-burner cooktop, two food-prep islands and a walk-in pantry, the gourmet kitchen easily serves planned events in the formal dining room, as well as impromptu fare in the leisure room. Nearby, a private vestibule leads to a guest suite that is secluded from two family bedrooms. A family valet, conveniently located, provides the perfect place to drop your keys and packages.

PLAN	*8061*

Bedroom: 4   Width: 68'8"
Bath: 3-1/2   Depth: 91'8"
Foundation: Slab
Exterior Walls: 8"CBS or 2x6

Main Level: 3,497 sq ft

Living Area: 3,497 sq ft

Price Code: **C4**

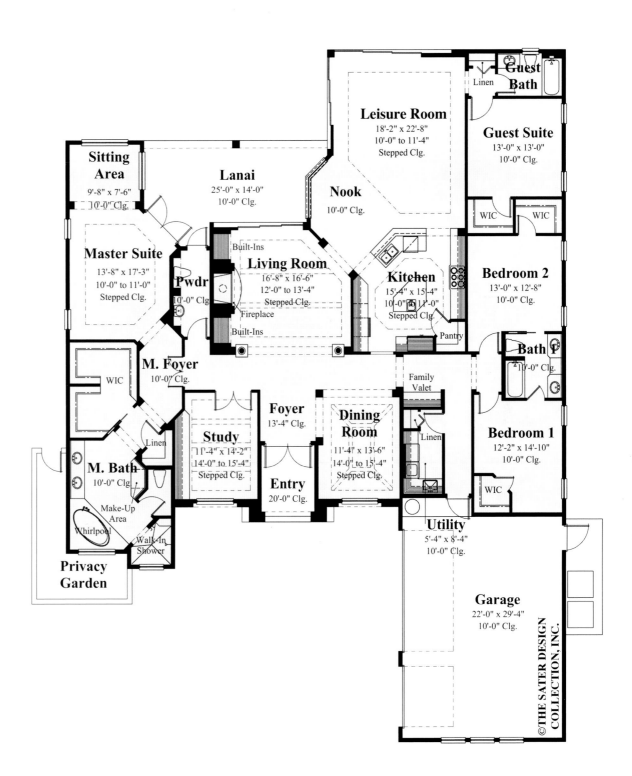

Sitting Area
9'-8" x 7'-6"
10'-0" Clg.

Lanai
25'-0" x 14'-0"
10'-0" Clg.

Leisure Room
18'-2" x 22'-8"
10'-0" to 11'-4"
Stepped Clg.

Guest Bath

Linen

Guest Suite
13'-0" x 13'-0"
10'-0" Clg.

Nook
10'-0" Clg.

Master Suite
13'-8" x 17'-3"
10'-0" to 11'-0"
Stepped Clg.

WIC WIC

Pwdr
10'-0" Clg

Living Room
16'-8" x 16'-6"
12'-0" to 13'-4"
Stepped Clg.

Built-Ins

Fireplace

Built-Ins

Kitchen
15'-4" x 15'-4"
10'-0" to 11'-0"
Stepped Clg.

Bedroom 2
13'-0" x 12'-8"
10'-0" Clg.

Pantry

M. Foyer
10'-0" Clg.

WIC

Bath 1
10'-0" Clg.

Linen

Family Valet

Linen

Study
11'-4" x 14'-2"
14'-0" to 15'-4"
Stepped Clg.

Foyer
13'-4" Clg.

Dining Room
11'-4" x 13'-6"
14'-0" to 15'-4"
Stepped Clg.

M. Bath
10'-0" Clg.

Entry
20'-0" Clg.

Bedroom 1
12'-2" x 14'-10"
10'-0" Clg.

Make-Up Area

Whirlpool

Walk-In Shower

WIC

Privacy Garden

Utility
5'-4" x 8'-4"
10'-0" Clg.

Garage
22'-0" x 29'-4"
10'-0" Clg.

©THE SATER DESIGN COLLECTION, INC.

rear elevation

About the Illustrator

DAVE JENKINS

With a career that spans nearly two decades, Dave Jenkins has produced thousands of renderings and sketches that grace the pages of publications sold across the globe. His work for Dan F. Sater, II, began in 1990, drawing custom homes for Sater Group and grew to Sater Design Collection plan books, such as the award-winning **Cottages** book. To this day, Dave has been Dan's illustrator-of-choice, and his extraordinary accomplishment is evident in the pages of this **European Luxury Home Plans** book.

"We may live in a hi-tech world with tract homes and 'virtual' tours, but Sater Design Collection still believes in creating homes that are uniquely beautiful and lasting. I believe in enhancing, not abandoning, time-tested traditions of quality design.

In this book, it was my hope to reflect this design philosophy in the renderings that would represent this, the latest effort of designer, Dan F. Sater, II.

All of the front rendering perspectives were created over a period of a year, drawn in pencil on vellum, the old-fashioned way. I enjoyed the process; I hope you enjoy the result." — Dave Jenkins

Art prints

You've found the perfect European plan — now you can have a beautiful rendering of your home to hang on your wall.

We are privileged to offer limited-edition prints exclusively to our valued clients. These high-resolution reproductions show amazing rendered detail, and come signed by award-winning illustrator Dave Jenkins. All are printed on archival acid-free, heavy-weight, watercolor paper, and are printed with pigmented inks for longevity. Each of these prints is truly a work of art suitable for framing. Each 15" x 22" piece comes with a certificate of authenticity and instructions on its care.
Price: $195.00 plus shipping.
Please allow 2 to 3 weeks for delivery.

More Plan Books | FROM SATER DESIGN COLLECTION, INC.

LUXURY—COASTAL/ MEDITERRANEAN BOOK

COUNTRY COMFORT FARMHOUSE BOOK

VACATION LUXURY HOMES MOUNTAIN, COTTAGE & VILLA

THE COTTAGES SEASIDE & TIDEWATER BOOK

LUXURY BOOK
49 superb plans featuring photo tours of magnificient luxury homes. Styles range from Mediterranean to Contemporary Coastal.
2,500-6,800 sq ft

$12.95
114 full-color pages and over 160 photos

COUNTRY COMFORT
75 elevations / 25 floor plans each with 3 styles: Classic, French Country & Victorian.
1,800-2,400 sq ft

$12.95
176 full-color pages

VACATION LUXURY HOMES: MOUNTAIN, COTTAGE & VILLA
63 elevations / 21 floor plans each with 3 styles: Mountain, Cottage & Villa.
1,300-4,300 sq ft

$10.00
144 full-color pages

THE COTTAGES
25 charming plans using raised Coastal and Tidewater styling. Artful detail that borrows freely from the past.
1,288-2,900 sq ft

$10.00
64 full-color pages

Each set of plans is a collection of drawings that show exactly how your house is to be built. Actual number of pages may vary, but most plan packages include the following:

A-1 COVER SHEET/INDEX & SITE PLAN

An Artist's Rendering of the exterior of the house shows you approximately how the house will look when built and landscaped. The Index is a list of the sheets included and page numbers for easy reference. The Site Plan is a scaled drawing of the house to help determine the placement of the home on a building site.

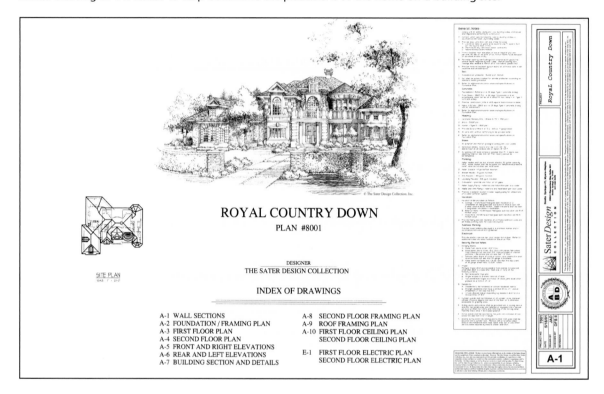

A-2 WALL SECTION / NOTES

This sheet shows details of the house from the roof to the foundation. This section specifies the home's construction, insulation, flooring and roofing details.

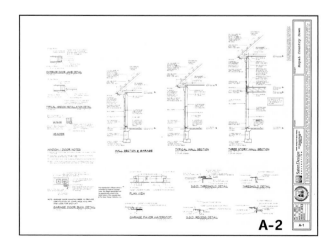

A-3 FOUNDATION PLAN

This sheet gives the foundation layout, including support walls, excavated and unexcavated areas, if any, and foundation notes. If the foundation is monolithic slab rather than basement, the plan shows footing and details.

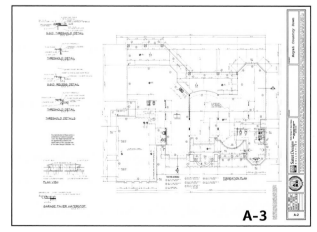

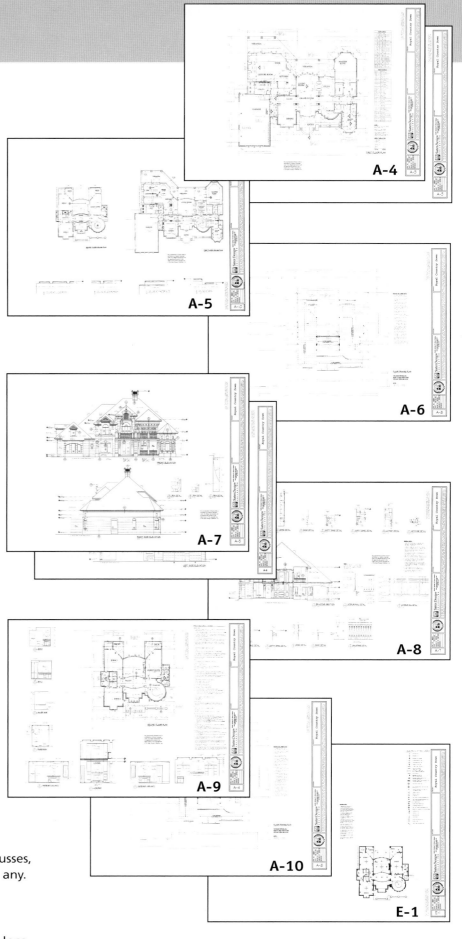

A-4 DETAILED FLOOR PLANS

These plans show the layout of each floor of the house. Rooms and interior spaces are carefully dimensioned and keys are given for cross-section details provided later in the plans, as well as window and door size call-outs. These plans also show the location of kitchen appliances and bathroom fixtures, etc.

A-5 CEILING PLAN

Sater ceiling treatments are typically very detailed. This plan shows ceiling layout and extensive details.

A-6 ROOF PLAN

Overall layout and necessary details for roof construction are provided. If trusses are used, we suggest using a local truss manufacturer to design your trusses to comply with your local codes and regulations.

A-7 EXTERIOR ELEVATIONS

Included are front, rear, left and right sides of the house. Exterior materials, details and measurements are also given.

A-8 CROSS SECTION & DETAILS

Important changes in floor, ceiling and roof heights or the relationship of one level to another are called out. Also shown, when applicable, are exterior details such as railing and banding.

A-9 INTERIOR ELEVATIONS

These plans show the specific details and design of cabinets, utility rooms, fireplaces, bookcases, built-in units and other special interior features depending on the nature and complexity of the item.

A-10 SECOND FLOOR FRAMING

This sheet shows directional spacing for floor trusses, beam locations and load-bearing conditions, if any.

E-1 ELECTRICAL PLAN

This sheet shows wiring and the suggested locations for switches, fixtures and outlets.

QUICK TURNAROUND

Because you are placing your order directly, we can ship plans to you quickly. If your order is placed before noon EST, we can usually have your plans to you the next business day. Some restrictions may apply. We cannot ship to a post office box; please provide a physical street address.

OUR EXCHANGE POLICY

Since our blueprints are printed especially for you at the time you place your order, we cannot accept any returns. If, for some reason, you find that the plan that you purchased does not meet your needs, then you may exchange that plan for another plan in our collection. We allow you sixty days from the time of purchase to make an exchange. At the time of the exchange, you will be charged a processing fee of 20% of the total amount of the original order plus the difference in price between the plans (if applicable) and the cost to ship the new plans to you. Vellums cannot be exchanged. All sets must be approved and authorization given before the exchange can take place. Please call our customer service department if you have any questions.

LOCAL BUILDING CODES AND ZONING REQUIREMENTS

Our plans are designed to meet or exceed national building standards. Because of the great differences in geography and climate, each state, county and municipality has its own building codes and zoning requirements. Your plan may need to be modified to comply with local requirements regarding snow loads, energy codes, soil and seismic conditions and a wide range of other matters. Prior to using plans ordered from us, we strongly advise that you consult a local building official.

ARCHITECTURE AND ENGINEERING SEALS

Some cities and states are now requiring that a licensed architect or engineer review and approve any set of building documents prior to construction. This is due to concerns over energy costs, safety, structural integrity and other factors. or to applying for a building permit or the start of actual construction, we strongly advise that you consult your local building official who can tell you if such a review is required.

DISCLAIMER

We have put substantial care and effort into the creation of our blueprints. We authorize the use of our blueprints on the express condition that you strictly comply with all local building codes, zoning requirements and other applicable laws, regulations and ordinances. However, because we cannot provide on-site consultation, supervision or control over actual construction, and because of the great variance in local building requirements, building practices and soil, seismic, weather and other conditions, WE CANNOT MAKE ANY WARRANTY, EXPRESS OR IMPLIED, WITH RESPECT TO THE CONTENT OR USE OF OUR BLUEPRINTS OR VELLUMS, INCLUDING BUT NOT LIMITED TO ANY WARRANTY OF MERCHANTABILITY OR OF FITNESS FOR A PARTICULAR PURPOSE. Please Note: Floor plans in this book are not construction documents and are subject to change. Renderings are artist's concept only.

HOW MANY SETS OF PRINTS WILL YOU NEED?

We offer a single set of prints so that you can study and plan your dream home in detail. However, you cannot build from this package. One set of blueprints is marked "NOT FOR CONSTRUCTION." If you are planning to get estimates from a contractor or subcontractor, or if you are planning to build immediately, you will need more sets. Because additional sets are less expensive, make sure you order enough to satisfy all your requirements. Sometimes changes are needed to a plan; in that case we offer vellums that are reproducible and erasable so changes can be made directly to the plans. Vellums are the only set that can be reproduced; it is illegal to copy blueprints. The checklist below will help you determine how many sets are needed.

Plan checklist

_____ **Owner** (one for notes, one for file)

_____ **Builder** (generally requires at least three sets; one as a legal document, one for inspections and at least one to give subcontractors)

_____ **Local Building Department** (often requires two sets)

_____ **Mortgage Lender** (usually one set for a conventional loan; three sets for FHA or VA loans)

_____ **Total Number of Sets**

IGNORING COPYRIGHT LAWS CAN BE A
$1,000,000 *mistake!*

Recent changes in the US copyright laws allow for statutory penalties of up to $150,000 per incident for copyright infringement involving any of the copyrighted plans found in this publication. The law can be confusing. So, for your own protection, take the time to understand what you can and cannot do when it comes to home plans.

WHAT YOU CAN'T DO!

YOU CANNOT DUPLICATE HOME PLANS

YOU CANNOT COPY ANY PART OF A HOME PLAN TO CREATE ANOTHER

YOU CANNOT BUILD A HOME WITHOUT BUYING A BLUEPRINT OR LICENSE

SATER DESIGN COLLECTION, INC.

25241 Elementary Way, Ste 201
Bonita Springs, FL 34135

1-800-718-7526

www.saterdesign.com

sales@saterdesign.com

ADDITIONAL ITEMS

11x17 Color Rendering Front Perspective	$195.00
Additional Blueprints (per set)	$65.00
Reverse Mirror-Image Blueprints	$50.00
Basement Plans*	$225.00
Pool Plans*	$225.00
Landscape Plans*	$200.00
Pool/Landscape Plans*	$375.00

*Call for availability. Special orders may require additional fees.

POSTAGE AND HANDLING

Overnight	$45.00
2nd Day	$35.00
Ground	$25.00
Saturday	$55.00

For shipping international, please call for a quote.

BLUEPRINT PRICE SCHEDULE*

	5 SETS	8 SETS	VELLUM
A2	$520	$560	$720
A3	$560	$600	$780
A4	$605	$645	$850
C1	$655	$700	$915
C2	$700	$745	$980
C3	$745	$790	$1050
C4	$795	$840	$1125
L1	$875	$925	$1240
L2	$950	$1000	$1350
L3	$1095	$1100	$1500
L4	$1150	$1200	$1650

* prices subject to change without notice

Order form

PLAN NUMBER _____

☐ 5-set building package .... $_____
☐ 8-set building package .... $_____
☐ 1-set of reproducible vellums .... $_____

____ Additional Identical Blueprints @ $65 each .... $_____
____ Reverse Mirror-Image Blueprints @ $50 fee .... $_____

Sub-Total $_____
Shipping and Handling $_____
Sales Tax (FL Res.) 6% $_____

TOTAL $_____

Check one: ☐ Visa ☐ MasterCard ☐ AmEx

Credit Card Number _____

Expiration Date _____

Signature _____

Name _____

Company _____

Street _____

City _____ State____ Zip_____

Daytime Telephone Number (____)_____

Check one:

☐ Consumer ☐ Builder ☐ Developer

European
LUXURY HOME PLANS

© The Sater Design Collection, Inc.

DESIGNED BY: Diane Zwack

ILLUSTRATED BY: Dave Jenkins

Set in Franklin Gothic and Bickham Script